REWORK

CHANGE THE WAY
YOU WORK FOREVER

Jason Fried and
David Heinemeier Hansson

Vermilion
LONDON

17

First published in the UK in 2010 by Vermilion, an imprint of Ebury Publishing
A Random House Group Company

Copyright © 37signals, LLC. 2010

Jason Fried and David Heinemeier Hansson
have asserted their right to be identified as the authors of this Work in
accordance with the Copyright, Designs and Patents Act 1988

The Random House Group Limited Reg. No. 954009

Addresses for companies within the Random House Group can be found at
www.randomhouse.co.uk

A CIP catalogue record for this book is available from the British Library

The Random House Group Limited supports the Forest Stewardship Council® (FSC®), the
leading international forest–certification organisation. Our books carrying the FSC label are
printed on FSC®–certified paper. FSC is the only forest–certification scheme supported by
the leading environmental organisations, including Greenpeace. Our paper procurement
policy can be found at www.randomhouse.co.uk/environment

MIX
Paper from
responsible sources
FSC® C016897

Printed and bound by CPI Group (UK) Ltd, Croydon, CR0 4YY

ISBN 9780091929787

Illustrations by Mike Rohde

To buy books by your favourite authors and register for offers visit
www.randomhouse.co.uk

INTRODUCTION 1

FIRST 7

The new reality 9

TAKEDOWNS 11

Ignore the real world 13

Learning from mistakes is overrated 16

Planning is guessing 19

Why grow? 22

Workaholism 25

Enough with "entrepreneurs" 28

GO 29

Make a dent in the universe 31

Scratch your own itch 34

Start making something 38

No time is no excuse 40

Draw a line in the sand   43

Mission statement impossible   47

Outside money is Plan Z   50

You need less than you think   53

Start a business, not a startup   56

Building to flip is building to flop   59

Less mass   62

PROGRESS   65

Embrace constraints   67

Build half a product, not a half-assed product   70

Start at the epicenter   72

Ignore the details early on   74

Making the call is making progress   77

Be a curator   80

Throw less at the problem   83

Focus on what won't change   85

Tone is in your fingers   87

Sell your by-products   90

Launch now   93

PRODUCTIVITY   95

Illusions of agreement   97

Reasons to quit   100

Interruption is the enemy of productivity   104

Meetings are toxic   108

CONTENTS v

Good enough is fine   112

Quick wins   115

Don't be a hero   118

Go to sleep   121

Your estimates suck   124

Long lists don't get done   127

Make tiny decisions   130

COMPETITORS   133

Don't copy   135

Decommoditize your product   138

Pick a fight   141

Underdo your competition   144

Who cares what they're doing?   148

EVOLUTION   151

Say no by default   153

Let your customers outgrow you   156

Don't confuse enthusiasm with priority   159

Be at-home good   161

Don't write it down   164

PROMOTION   165

Welcome obscurity   167

Build an audience   170

Out-teach your competition   173

Emulate chefs   176

Go behind the scenes   179

Nobody likes plastic flowers   182

Press releases are spam   185

Forget about the *Wall Street Journal*   188

Drug dealers get it right   191

Marketing is not a department   193

The myth of the overnight sensation   196

HIRING   199

Do it yourself first   201

Hire when it hurts   204

Pass on great people   206

Strangers at a cocktail party   208

Resumés are ridiculous   210

Years of irrelevance   213

Forget about formal education   215

Everybody works   218

Hire managers of one   220

Hire great writers   222

The best are everywhere   224

Test-drive employees   227

DAMAGE CONTROL   229

Own your bad news   231

Speed changes everything   235

How to say you're sorry   238

Put everyone on the front lines   241

Take a deep breath   244

CULTURE   247

You don't create a culture   249

Decisions are temporary   251

Skip the rock stars   253

They're not thirteen   255

Send people home at 5   258

Don't scar on the first cut   260

Sound like you   262

Four-letter words   265

ASAP is poison   268

CONCLUSION   269

Inspiration is perishable   271

RESOURCES   275

About 37signals   277

37signals products   278

ACKNOWLEDGMENTS   279

CHAPTER

INTRODUCTION

We have something new to say about building, running, and growing (or not growing) a business.

This book isn't based on academic theories. It's based on our experience. We've been in business for more than ten years. Along the way, we've seen two recessions, one burst bubble, business-model shifts, and doom-and-gloom predictions come and go—and we've remained profitable through it all.

We're an intentionally small company that makes software to help small companies and groups get things done the easy way. More than 3 million people around the world use our products.

We started out in 1999 as a three-person Web-design consulting firm. In 2004, we weren't happy with the project-management software used by the rest of the industry, so we created our own: Basecamp. When we showed the online tool to clients and colleagues, they all said the same thing: "We need this for our business too." Five years later, Basecamp generates millions of dollars a year in profits.

We now sell other online tools too. Highrise, our contact manager and simple CRM (customer relationship management) tool, is used by tens of thousands of small businesses to keep track of leads, deals, and more than 10 million contacts. More than 500,000 people have signed up for Backpack, our intranet and knowledge-sharing tool. And people have sent more than 100 million messages using Campfire, our real-time business chat tool. We also invented and open-sourced a computer-programming framework called Ruby on Rails that powers much of the Web 2.0 world.

Some people consider us an Internet company, but that makes us cringe. Internet companies are known for hiring compulsively, spending wildly, and failing spectacularly. That's not us. We're small (sixteen people as this book goes to press), frugal, and profitable.

A lot of people say we can't do what we do. They call us a fluke. They advise others to ignore our advice. Some have even called us irresponsible, reckless, and— gasp!—unprofessional.

These critics don't understand how a company can reject growth, meetings, budgets, boards of directors, advertising, salespeople, and "the real world," yet thrive. That's their problem, not ours. They say you need to sell to the Fortune 500. Screw that. We sell to the Fortune 5,000,000.

They don't think you can have employees who almost never see each other spread out across eight cities on two continents. They say you can't succeed without making financial projections and five-year plans. They're wrong.

They say you need a PR firm to make it into the pages of *Time, BusinessWeek, Inc., Fast Company*, the *New York Times*, the *Financial Times*, the *Chicago Tribune*, the *Atlantic, Entrepreneur,* and *Wired*. They're wrong. They say you can't share your recipes and bare your secrets and still withstand the competition. Wrong again.

They say you can't possibly compete with the big boys without a hefty marketing and advertising budget. They say you can't succeed by building products that do less than your competition's. They say you can't make it all up as you go. But that's exactly what we've done.

They say a lot of things. We say they're wrong. We've *proved* it. And we wrote this book to show you how to prove them wrong too.

First, we'll start out by gutting business. We'll take it down to the studs and explain why it's time to throw out the traditional notions of what it takes to run a business. Then we'll rebuild it. You'll learn how to begin, why you need less than you think, when to launch, how to get the word out, whom (and when) to hire, and how to keep it all under control.

Now, let's get on with it.

CHAPTER
FIRST

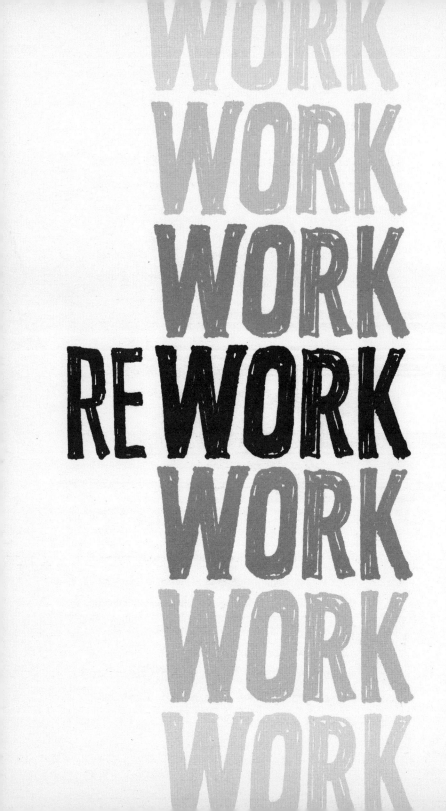

The new reality

This is a different kind of business book for different kinds of people—from those who have never dreamed of starting a business to those who already have a successful company up and running.

It's for hard-core entrepreneurs, the Type A go-getters of the business world. People who feel like they were born to start, lead, and conquer.

It's also for less intense small-business owners. People who may not be Type A but still have their business at the center of their lives. People who are looking for an edge that'll help them do more, work smarter, and kick ass.

It's even for people stuck in day jobs who have always dreamed about doing their own thing. Maybe they like what they do, but they don't like their boss. Or maybe they're just bored. They want to do something they love and get paid for it.

Finally, it's for all those people who've never considered going out on their own and starting a business. Maybe they don't think they're cut out for it. Maybe they don't think they have the time, money, or conviction to see it through. Maybe they're just afraid of putting themselves on the line. Or maybe they just think *business* is a dirty word. Whatever the reason, this book is for them, too.

There's a new reality. Today anyone can be in business. Tools that used to be out of reach are now easily accessible. Technology that cost thousands is now just a few bucks or even free. One person can do the job of two or three or, in some cases, an entire department. Stuff that was impossible just a few years ago is simple today.

You don't have to work miserable 60/80/100-hour weeks to make it work. 10–40 hours a week is plenty. You don't have to deplete your life savings or take on a boatload of risk. Starting a business on the side while keeping your day job can provide all the cash flow you need. You don't even need an office. Today you can work from home or collaborate with people you've never met who live thousands of miles away.

It's time to rework work. Let's get started.

CHAPTER

TAKEDOWNS

Ignore the real world

"That would never work in the real world." You hear it all the time when you tell people about a fresh idea.

This real world sounds like an awfully depressing place to live. It's a place where new ideas, unfamiliar approaches, and foreign concepts *always* lose. The only things that win are what people already know and do, even if those things are flawed and inefficient.

Scratch the surface and you'll find these "real world" inhabitants are filled with pessimism and despair. They expect fresh concepts to fail. They assume society isn't ready for or capable of change.

Even worse, they want to drag others down into their tomb. If you're hopeful and ambitious, they'll try to convince you your ideas are impossible. They'll say you're wasting your time.

Don't believe them. That world may be real for them, but it doesn't mean you have to live in it.

We know because our company fails the real-world test in all kinds of ways. In the real world, you can't have more than a dozen employees spread out in eight different cities on two continents. In the real world, you can't attract millions of customers without any salespeople or advertising. In the real world, you can't reveal your formula for success to the rest of the world. But we've done all those things and prospered.

The real world isn't a place, it's an excuse. It's a justification for not trying. It has nothing to do with you.

Learning from mistakes is overrated

In the business world, failure has become an expected rite of passage. You hear all the time how nine out of ten new businesses fail. You hear that your business's chances are slim to none. You hear that failure builds character. People advise, "Fail early and fail often."

With so much failure in the air, you can't help but breathe it in. Don't inhale. Don't get fooled by the stats. Other people's failures are just that: *other* people's failures.

If other people can't market their product, it has nothing to do with you. If other people can't build a team, it has nothing to do with you. If other people can't price their services properly, it has nothing to do with you. If other people can't earn more than they spend . . . well, you get it.

Another common misconception: You need to learn from your mistakes. What do you really learn from mistakes? You might learn what *not* to do again, but how valuable is that? You still don't know what you *should* do next.

Contrast that with learning from your successes. Success gives you real ammunition. When something succeeds, you know what worked—and you can do it again. And the next time, you'll probably do it even better.

Failure is not a prerequisite for success. A Harvard Business School study found already-successful entrepreneurs are far more likely to succeed again (the success rate for their future companies is 34 percent). But entrepreneurs whose companies failed the first time had almost the same follow-on success rate as people starting a company for the first time: just 23 percent. People who failed before have the same amount of success as people who have never tried at all.* Success is the experience that actually counts.

That shouldn't be a surprise: It's exactly how nature works. Evolution doesn't linger on past failures, it's always building upon what worked. So should you.

---

*Leslie Berlin, "Try, Try Again, or Maybe Not," *New York Times,* Mar. 21, 2009.

Planning is guessing

Unless you're a fortune-teller, long-term business planning is a fantasy. There are just too many factors that are out of your hands: market conditions, competitors, customers, the economy, etc. Writing a plan makes you feel in control of things you can't actually control.

Why don't we just call plans what they really are: guesses. Start referring to your business plans as business guesses, your financial plans as financial guesses, and your strategic plans as strategic guesses. Now you can stop worrying about them as much. They just aren't worth the stress.

When you turn guesses into plans, you enter a danger zone. Plans let the past drive the future. They put blinders on you. "This is where we're going because, well, that's where we said we were going." And that's the problem: Plans are inconsistent with improvisation.

And you have to be able to improvise. You have to be able to pick up opportunities that come along. Sometimes you need to say, "We're going in a new direction because that's what makes sense *today*."

The timing of long-range plans is screwed up too. You have the most information when you're doing something, not *before* you've done it. Yet when do you write a plan? Usually it's before you've even begun. That's the worst time to make a big decision.

Now this isn't to say you shouldn't think about the future or contemplate how you might attack upcoming obstacles. That's a worthwhile exercise. Just don't feel you need to write it down or obsess about it. If you write a big plan, you'll most likely never look at it anyway. Plans more than a few pages long just wind up as fossils in your file cabinet.

Give up on the guesswork. Decide what you're going to do this week, not this year. Figure out the next most important thing and do that. Make decisions right before you do something, not far in advance.

It's OK to wing it. Just get on the plane and go. You can pick up a nicer shirt, shaving cream, and a toothbrush once you get there.

Working without a plan may seem scary. But blindly following a plan that has no relationship with reality is even scarier.

GROW GROW GROW GROW GROW GROW

→ WHY?

Why grow?

People ask, "How big is your company?" It's small talk, but they're not looking for a small answer. The bigger the number, the more impressive, professional, and powerful you sound. "Wow, nice!" they'll say if you have a hundred-plus employees. If you're small, you'll get an "*Oh* . . . that's nice." The former is meant as a compliment; the latter is said just to be polite.

Why is that? What is it about growth and business? Why is expansion always the goal? What's the attraction of big besides ego? (You'll need a better answer than "economies of scale.") What's wrong with finding the right size and staying there?

Do we look at Harvard or Oxford and say, "If they'd only expand and branch out and hire thousands more professors and go global and open other campuses all over the world . . . *then* they'd be great schools." Of course not. That's not how we measure the value of these institutions. So why is it the way we measure businesses?

Maybe the right size for your company is five people. Maybe it's forty. Maybe it's two hundred. Or maybe it's just you and a laptop. Don't make assumptions about how big you should be ahead of time. Grow slow and see what feels right—premature hiring is the death of many companies. And avoid huge growth spurts too—they can cause you to skip right over your appropriate size.

Small is not just a stepping-stone. Small is a great destination in itself.

Have you ever noticed that while small businesses wish they were bigger, big businesses dream about being more agile and flexible? And remember, once you get big, it's really hard to shrink without firing people, damaging morale, and changing the entire way you do business.

Ramping up doesn't have to be your goal. And we're not talking just about the number of employees you have either. It's also true for expenses, rent, IT infrastructure, furniture, etc. These things don't just happen to you. You decide whether or not to take them on. And if you do take them on, you'll be taking on new headaches, too. Lock in lots of expenses and you force yourself into building a complex businesss—one that's a lot more difficult and stressful to run.

Don't be insecure about aiming to be a small business. Anyone who runs a business that's sustainable and profitable, whether it's big or small, should be proud.

Workaholism

Our culture celebrates the idea of the workaholic. We hear about people burning the midnight oil. They pull all-nighters and sleep at the office. It's considered a badge of honor to kill yourself over a project. No amount of work is too much work.

Not only is this workaholism unnecessary, it's stupid. Working more doesn't mean you care more or get more done. It just means you work more.

Workaholics wind up creating more problems than they solve. First off, working like that just isn't sustainable over time. When the burnout crash comes—and it will—it'll hit that much harder.

Workaholics miss the point, too. They try to fix problems by throwing sheer hours at them. They try to make up for intellectual laziness with brute force. This results in inelegant solutions.

They even create crises. They don't look for ways to be more efficient because they actually *like* working overtime. They enjoy feeling like heroes. They create problems (often unwittingly) just so they can get off on working more.

Workaholics make the people who don't stay late feel inadequate for "merely" working reasonable hours. That leads to guilt and poor morale all around. Plus, it leads to an ass-in-seat mentality—people stay late out of obligation, even if they aren't really being productive.

If all you do is work, you're unlikely to have sound judgments. Your values and decision making wind up skewed. You stop being able to decide what's worth extra effort and what's not. And you wind up just plain tired. No one makes sharp decisions when tired.

In the end, workaholics don't actually accomplish more than nonworkaholics. They may claim to be perfectionists, but that just means they're wasting time fixating on inconsequential details instead of moving on to the next task.

Workaholics aren't heroes. They don't save the day, they just use it up. The real hero is already home because she figured out a faster way to get things done.

BE a STARTER!

Enough with "entrepreneurs"

Let's retire the term *entrepreneur*. It's outdated and loaded with baggage. It smells like a members-only club. Everyone should be encouraged to start his own business, not just some rare breed that self-identifies as entrepreneurs.

There's a new group of people out there starting businesses. They're turning profits yet never think of themselves as entrepreneurs. A lot of them don't even think of themselves as business owners. They are just doing what they love on their own terms and getting paid for it.

So let's replace the fancy-sounding word with something a bit more down-to-earth. Instead of entrepreneurs, let's just call them starters. Anyone who creates a new business is a starter. You don't need an MBA, a certificate, a fancy suit, a briefcase, or an above-average tolerance for risk. You just need an idea, a touch of confidence, and a push to get started.

CHAPTER

Make a dent in the universe

To do great work, you need to feel that you're making a difference. That you're putting a meaningful dent in the universe. That you're part of something important.

This doesn't mean you need to find the cure for cancer. It's just that your efforts need to feel valuable. You want your customers to say, "This makes my life better." You want to feel that if you stopped doing what you do, people would notice.

You should feel an urgency about this too. You don't have forever. This is your life's work. Do you want to build just another me-too product or do you want to shake things up? What you do is your legacy. Don't sit around and wait for someone else to make the change you want to see. And don't think it takes a huge team to make that difference either.

Look at Craigslist, which demolished the traditional classified-ad business. With just a few dozen employees, the company generates tens of millions in revenue, has one of the most popular sites on the Internet, and disrupted the entire newspaper business.

The Drudge Report, run by Matt Drudge, is just one simple page on the Web run by one guy. Yet it's had a huge impact on the news industry—television producers, radio talk show hosts and newspaper reporters routinely view it as the go-to place for new stories.*

If you're going to do something, do something that matters. These little guys came out of nowhere and destroyed old models that had been around for decades. You can do the same in your industry.

---

*Jim Rutenberg, "Clinton Finds Way to Play Along with Drudge," *New York Times,* Oct. 22, 2007.

Scratch your own itch

The easiest, most straightforward way to create a great product or service is to make something *you* want to use. That lets you design what you know—and you'll figure out immediately whether or not what you're making is any good.

At 37signals, we build products we need to run our own business. For example, we wanted a way to keep track of whom we talked to, what we said, and when we need to follow up next. So we created Highrise, our contact-management software. There was no need for focus groups, market studies, or middlemen. We had the itch, so we scratched it.

When you build a product or service, you make the call on hundreds of tiny decisions each day. If you're solving someone else's problem, you're constantly stabbing in the dark. When you solve your own problem, the light comes on. You know exactly what the right answer is.

Inventor James Dyson scratched his own itch. While vacuuming his home, he realized his bag vacuum cleaner was constantly losing suction power—dust kept clogging the pores in the bag and blocking the airflow. It wasn't someone else's *imaginary* problem; it was a real one that he experienced firsthand. So he decided to solve the problem and came up with the world's first cyclonic, bagless vacuum cleaner.*

Vic Firth came up with the idea of making a better drumstick while playing timpani for the Boston Symphony Orchestra. The sticks he could buy commercially didn't measure up to the job, so he began making and selling drumsticks from his basement at home. Then one day he dropped a bunch of sticks on the floor and heard all the different pitches. That's when he began to match up sticks by moisture content, weight, density, and pitch so they were identical pairs. The result became his product's tag line: "the perfect pair." Today, Vic Firth's factory turns out more than 85,000 drumsticks a day and has a 62 percent share in the drumstick market.†

Track coach Bill Bowerman decided that his team needed better, lighter running shoes. So he went out to his workshop and poured rubber into the family waffle iron. That's how Nike's famous waffle sole was born.‡

These people scratched their own itch and exposed

---

*"Fascinating Facts About James Dyson, Inventor of the Dyson Vacuum Cleaner in 1978," www.ideafinder.com/history/inventors/dyson.htm
†Russ Mitchell, "The Beat Goes On," CBS News, *Sunday Morning*, Mar. 29, 2009, www.tinyurl.com/cd8gjq
‡Eric Ransdell, "The Nike Story? Just Tell It!" *Fast Company*, Dec. 19, 2007, www.fastcompany.com/magazine/31/nike.html

a huge market of people who needed exactly what they needed. That's how you should do it too.

When you build what *you* need, you can also assess the quality of what you make quickly and directly, instead of by proxy.

Mary Kay Wagner, founder of Mary Kay Cosmetics, knew her skin-care products were great because she used them herself. She got them from a local cosmetologist who sold homemade formulas to patients, relatives, and friends. When the cosmetologist passed away, Wagner bought the formulas from the family. She didn't need focus groups or studies to know the products were good. She just had to look at her own skin.*

Best of all, this "solve your own problem" approach lets you fall in love with what you're making. You know the problem and the value of its solution intimately. There's no substitute for that. After all, you'll (hopefully) be working on this for years to come. Maybe even the rest of your life. It better be something you really care about.

---

*"Mary Kay Ash: Mary Kay Cosmetics," *Journal of Business Leadership* 1, no. 1 (Spring 1988); American National Business Hall of Fame, www.anbhf.org/laureates/mkash.html

Start making something

We all have that one friend who says, "I had the idea for eBay. If only I had acted on it, I'd be a billionaire!" That logic is pathetic and delusional. Having the idea for eBay has nothing to do with actually creating eBay. What you *do* is what matters, not what you think or say or plan.

Think your idea's that valuable? Then go try to sell it and see what you get for it. *Not much* is probably the answer. Until you actually start making something, your brilliant idea is just that, an idea. And everyone's got one of those.

Stanley Kubrick gave this advice to aspiring filmmakers: "Get hold of a camera and some film and make a movie of any kind at all."* Kubrick knew that when you're new at something, you need to start creating. The most important thing is to begin. So get a camera, hit Record, and start shooting.

Ideas are cheap and plentiful. The original pitch idea is such a small part of a business that it's almost negligible. The real question is how well you execute.

---

*"*Stanley Kubrick*—Biography," IMDB,
www.imdb.com/name/nm0000040/bio

No time is no excuse

The most common excuse people give: "There's not enough time." They claim they'd love to start a company, learn an instrument, market an invention, write a book, or whatever, but there just aren't enough hours in the day.

Come on. There's always enough time if you spend it right. And don't think you have to quit your day job, either. Hang onto it and start work on your project at night.

Instead of watching TV or playing World of Warcraft, work on your idea. Instead of going to bed at ten, go to bed at eleven. We're not talking about all-nighters or sixteen-hour days—we're talking about squeezing out a few extra hours a week. That's enough time to get something going.

Once you do that, you'll learn whether your excitement and interest is real or just a passing phase. If it doesn't pan out, you just keep going to work every day like you've been doing all along. You didn't risk or lose anything, other than a bit of time, so it's no big deal.

When you want something bad enough, you make the time—regardless of your other obligations. The truth is most people just don't want it bad enough. Then they protect their ego with the excuse of time.

Don't let yourself off the hook with excuses. It's entirely your responsibility to make your dreams come true.

Besides, the *perfect* time never arrives. You're always too young or old or busy or broke or something else. If you constantly fret about timing things perfectly, they'll never happen.

Draw a line in the sand

As you get going, keep in mind *why* you're doing what you're doing. Great businesses have a point of view, not just a product or service. You have to believe in something. You need to have a backbone. You need to know what you're willing to fight for. And then you need to show the world.

A strong stand is how you attract superfans. They point to you and defend you. And they spread the word further, wider, and more passionately than any advertising could.

Strong opinions aren't free. You'll turn some people off. They'll accuse you of being arrogant and aloof. That's life. For everyone who loves you, there will be others who hate you. If no one's upset by what you're saying, you're probably not pushing hard enough. (And you're probably boring, too.)

Lots of people hate us because our products do less than the competition's. They're insulted when we refuse to include their pet feature. But we're just as proud of what our products don't do as we are of what they do.

We design them to be simple because we believe most software is too complex: too many features, too many buttons, too much confusion. So we build software that's the opposite of that. If what we make isn't right for everyone, that's OK. We're willing to lose some customers if it means that others love our products intensely. That's our line in the sand.

When you don't know what you believe, everything becomes an argument. Everything is debatable. But when you stand for something, decisions are obvious.

For example, Whole Foods stands for selling the highest quality natural and organic products available. They don't waste time deciding over and over again what's appropriate. No one asks, "Should we sell this product that has artificial flavors?" There's no debate. The answer is clear. That's why you can't buy a Coke or a Snickers there.

This belief means the food is more expensive at Whole Foods. Some haters even call it Whole Paycheck and make fun of those who shop there. But so what? Whole Foods is doing pretty damn well.

Another example is Vinnie's Sub Shop, just down the street from our office in Chicago. They put this homemade basil oil on subs that's just perfect. You better show up on time, though. Ask when they close and the woman behind the counter will respond, "We close when the bread runs out."

Really? "Yeah. We get our bread from the bakery down the street early in the morning, when it's the freshest. Once we run out (usually around two or three p.m.), we close up shop. We could get more bread later in the day, but it's not as good as the fresh-baked bread in the morning. There's no point in selling a few more sandwiches if the bread isn't good. A few bucks isn't going to make up for selling food we can't be proud of."

Wouldn't you rather eat at a place like that instead of some generic sandwich chain?

Mission statement impossible

There's a world of difference between truly standing for something and having a mission statement that *says* you stand for something. You know, those "providing the best service" signs that are created just to be posted on a wall. The ones that sound phony and disconnected from reality.

Imagine you're standing in a rental-car office. The room's cold. The carpet is dirty. There's no one at the counter. And then you see a tattered piece of paper with some clip art at the top of it pinned to a bulletin board. It's a mission statement:

> Our mission is to fulfill the automotive and commercial truck rental, leasing, car sales and related needs of our customers and, in doing so, exceed their expectations for service, quality and value.
>
> We will strive to earn our customers' long-term loyalty by working to deliver more than promised, being honest and fair and "going the extra mile" to provide exceptional personalized service that creates a pleasing business experience.
>
> We must motivate our employees to provide exceptional service to our customers by supporting their development, providing opportunities for

personal growth and fairly compensating them for
their successes and achievements . . . *

And it drones on. And you're sitting there reading this crap and wondering, "What kind of idiot do they take me for?" The words on the paper are clearly disconnected from the reality of the experience.

It's like when you're on hold and a recorded voice comes on telling you how much the company values you as a customer. Really? Then maybe you should hire some more support people so I don't have to wait thirty minutes to get help.

Or just say nothing. But don't give me an automated voice that's telling me how much you care about me. It's a robot. I know the difference between genuine affection and a robot that's programmed to say nice things.

Standing for something isn't just about writing it down. It's about believing it and living it.

---

*Mission, Enterprise Rent-a-Car,
http://aboutus.enterprise.com/who_we_are/mission.html

Outside money is Plan Z

One of the first questions you'll probably ask: Where's the seed money going to come from? Far too often, people think the answer is to raise money from outsiders. If you're building something like a factory or restaurant, then you may indeed need that outside cash. But a lot of companies don't need expensive infrastructure—especially these days.

We're in a service economy now. Service businesses (e.g., consultants, software companies, wedding planners, graphic designers, and hundreds of others) don't require much to get going. If you're running a business like that, avoid outside funding.

In fact, no matter what kind of business you're starting, take on as little outside cash as you can. Spending other people's money may sound great, but there's a noose attached. Here's why:

You give up control. When you turn to outsiders for funding, you have to answer to them too. That's fine at first, when everyone agrees. But what happens down the road? Are you starting your own business to take orders from someone else? Raise money and that's what you'll wind up doing.

"Cashing out" begins to trump building a quality business. Investors want their money back—and quickly (usually three to five years). Long-term sustainability goes out the window when those involved only want to cash out as soon as they can.

Spending other people's money is addictive.
There's nothing easier than spending other people's
money. But then you run out and need to go back
for more. And every time you go back, they take
more of your company.

It's usually a bad deal. When you're just beginning, you have no leverage. That's a terrible time to
enter into any financial transaction.

Customers move down the totem pole. You wind
up building what *investors* want instead of what *customers* want.

Raising money is incredibly distracting. Seeking
funding is difficult and draining. It takes months of
pitch meetings, legal maneuvering, contracts, etc.
That's an enormous distraction when you should
really be focused on building something great.

It's just not worth it. We hear over and over from business owners who have gone down this road and regret it.
They usually give a variation on the investment-hangover
story: First, you get that quick investment buzz. But then
you start having meetings with your investors and/or
board of directors, and you're like, "Oh man, what have I
gotten myself into?" Now someone else is calling the shots.

Before you stick your head in that noose, look for
another way.

You need less than you think

Do you really need ten people or will two or three do for now?

Do you really need $500,000 or is $50,000 (or $5,000) enough for now?

Do you really need six months or can you make something in two?

Do you really need a big office or can you share office space (or work from home) for a while?

Do you really need a warehouse or can you rent a small storage space (or use your garage or basement) or outsource it completely?

Do you really need to buy advertising and hire a PR firm or are there other ways to get noticed?

Do you really need to build a factory or can you hire someone else to manufacture your products?

Do you really need an accountant or can you use Quicken and do it yourself?

Do you really need an IT department or can you outsource it?

Do you really need a full-time support person or can you handle inquiries on your own?

Do you really need to open a retail store or can you sell your product online?

Do you really need fancy business cards, letterhead, and brochures or can you forego that stuff?

You get the point. Maybe eventually you'll need to go the bigger, more expensive route, but not right now.

There's nothing wrong with being frugal. When we launched our first product, we did it on the cheap. We didn't get our own office; we shared space with another company. We didn't get a bank of servers; we had only one. We didn't advertise; we promoted by sharing our experiences online. We didn't hire someone to answer customer e-mails; the company founder answered them himself. And everything worked out just fine.

Great companies start in garages all the time. Yours can too.

Start a business, not a startup

Ah, the startup. It's a special breed of company that gets a lot of attention (especially in the tech world).

The startup is a magical place. It's a place where expenses are someone else's problem. It's a place where that pesky thing called revenue is never an issue. It's a place where you can spend other people's money until you figure out a way to make your own. It's a place where the laws of business physics don't apply.

The problem with this magical place is it's a fairy tale. The truth is every business, new or old, is governed by the same set of market forces and economic rules. Revenue in, expenses out. Turn a profit or wind up gone.

Startups try to ignore this reality. They are run by people trying to postpone the inevitable, i.e., that moment when their business has to grow up, turn a profit, and be a real, sustainable business.

Anyone who takes a "we'll figure out how to profit in the future" attitude to business is being ridiculous. That's like building a rocket ship but starting off by saying, "Let's pretend gravity doesn't exist." *A business without a path to profit isn't a business, it's a hobby.*

So don't use the idea of a startup as a crutch. Instead, start an actual business. Actual businesses have to deal with actual things like bills and payroll. Actual businesses worry about profit from day one. Actual businesses don't mask deep problems by saying, "It's OK, we're a startup." Act like an actual business and you'll have a much better shot at succeeding.

Building to flip is building to flop

Another thing you hear a lot: "What's your exit strategy?" You hear it even when you're just beginning. What is it with people who can't even start building something without knowing how they're going to leave it? What's the hurry? Your priorities are out of whack if you're thinking about getting out before you even dive in.

Would you go into a relationship planning the breakup? Would you write the prenup on a first date? Would you meet with a divorce lawyer the morning of your wedding? That would be ridiculous, right?

You need a commitment strategy, not an exit strategy. You should be thinking about how to make your project grow and succeed, not how you're going to jump ship. If your whole strategy is based on leaving, chances are you won't get far in the first place.

You see so many aspiring businesspeople pinning their hopes on selling out. But the odds of getting acquired are so tiny. There's only a slim chance that some big suitor will come along and make it all worthwhile. Maybe 1 in 1,000? Or 1 in 10,000?

Plus, when you build a company with the intention of being acquired, you emphasize the wrong things. Instead of focusing on getting customers to love you, you worry about who's going to buy you. That's the wrong thing to obsess over.

And let's say you ignore this advice and do pull off a flip. You build your business, sell it, and get a nice payday. Then what? Move to an island and sip piña coladas all day? Will that really satisfy you? Will money alone truly make you happy? Are you sure you'll like that more than running a business you actually enjoy and believe in?

That's why you often hear about business owners who sell out, retire for six months, and then get back in the game. They miss the thing they gave away. And usually, they're back with a business that isn't nearly as good as their first.

Don't be that guy. If you do manage to get a good thing going, keep it going. Good things don't come around that often. Don't let your business be the one that got away.

Less mass

Embrace the idea of having less mass. Right now, you're the smallest, the leanest, and the fastest you'll ever be. From here on out, you'll start accumulating mass. And the more massive an object, the more energy required to change its direction. It's as true in the business world as it is in the physical world.

Mass is increased by . . .

- Long-term contracts
- Excess staff
- Permanent decisions
- Meetings
- Thick process
- Inventory (physical or mental)
- Hardware, software, and technology lock-ins
- Long-term road maps
- Office politics

Avoid these things whenever you can. That way, you'll be able to change direction easily. The more expensive it is to make a change, the less likely you are to make it.

Huge organizations can take years to pivot. They talk instead of act. They meet instead of do. But if you keep your mass low, you can quickly change anything: your entire business model, product, feature set, and/or marketing message. You can make mistakes and fix them quickly. You can change your priorities, product mix, or focus. And most important, you can change your mind.

CHAPTER

PROGRESS

LESS IS A GOOD THING

Embrace constraints

"I don't have enough time/money/people/experience." Stop whining. Less is a good thing. Constraints are advantages in disguise. Limited resources force you to make do with what you've got. There's no room for waste. And that forces you to be creative.

Ever seen the weapons prisoners make out of soap or a spoon? They make do with what they've got. Now we're not saying you should go out and shank somebody—but get creative and you'll be amazed at what you can make with just a little.

Writers use constraints to force creativity all the time. Shakespeare reveled in the limitations of sonnets (fourteen-line lyric poems in iambic pentameter with a specific rhyme scheme). Haiku and limericks also have strict rules that lead to creative results. Writers like Ernest Hemingway and Raymond Carver found that forcing themselves to use simple, clear language helped them deliver maximum impact.

The Price Is Right, the longest-running game show in history, is also a great example of creativity born from embracing constraints. The show has more than a hundred games, and each one is based on the question "How much does this item cost?" That simple formula has attracted fans for more than thirty years.

Southwest—unlike most other airlines, which fly multiple aircraft models—flies only Boeing 737s. As a result, every Southwest pilot, flight attendant, and ground-crew member can work any flight. Plus, all of Southwest's parts fit all of its planes. All that means lower costs and a business that's easier to run. They made it easy on themselves.

When we were building Basecamp, we had plenty of limitations. We had a design firm to run with existing client work, a seven-hour time difference between principals (David was doing the programming in Denmark, the rest of us were in the States), a small team, and no outside funding. These constraints forced us to keep the product simple.

These days, we have more resources and people, but we still force constraints. We make sure to have only one or two people working on a product at a time. And we always keep features to a minimum. Boxing ourselves in this way prevents us from creating bloated products.

So before you sing the "not enough" blues, see how far you can get with what you have.

YOU'RE BETTER OFF with a KICK-ASS HALF than a HALF-ASSED WHOLE

Build half a product, not a half-assed product

You can turn a bunch of great ideas into a crappy product real fast by trying to do them all at once. You just can't do *everything* you want to do and do it well. You have limited time, resources, ability, and focus. It's hard enough to do one thing right. Trying to do ten things well at the same time? Forget about it.

So sacrifice some of your darlings for the greater good. Cut your ambition in half. You're better off with a kick-ass half than a half-assed whole.

Most of your great ideas won't seem all that great once you get some perspective, anyway. And if they truly are that fantastic, you can always do them later.

Lots of things get better as they get shorter. Directors cut good scenes to make a great movie. Musicians drop good tracks to make a great album. Writers eliminate good pages to make a great book. We cut this book in half between the next-to-last and final drafts. From 57,000 words to about 27,000 words. Trust us, it's better for it.

So start chopping. Getting to great starts by cutting out stuff that's merely good.

Start at the epicenter

When you start anything new, there are forces pulling you in a variety of directions. There's the stuff you *could* do, the stuff you *want* to do, and the stuff you *have* to do. The stuff you *have* to do is where you should begin. Start at the epicenter.

For example, if you're opening a hot dog stand, you could worry about the condiments, the cart, the name, the decoration. But the first thing you should worry about is the hot dog. The hot dogs are the epicenter. Everything else is secondary.

The way to find the epicenter is to ask yourself this question: "If I took this away, would what I'm selling still exist?" A hot dog stand isn't a hot dog stand without the hot dogs. You can take away the onions, the relish, the mustard, etc. Some people may not like your toppings-less dogs, but you'd still have a hot dog stand. But you simply cannot have a hot dog stand without any hot dogs.

So figure out your epicenter. Which part of your equation can't be removed? If you can continue to get by without this thing or that thing, then those things aren't the epicenter. When you find it, you'll know. Then focus all your energy on making it the best it can be. Everything else you do depends on that foundation.

Ignore the details early on

Architects don't worry about which tiles go in the shower or which brand of dishwasher to install in the kitchen until *after* the floor plan is finalized. They know it's better to decide these details later.

You need to approach your idea the same way. Details make the difference. But getting infatuated with details too early leads to disagreement, meetings, and delays. You get lost in things that don't really matter. You waste time on decisions that are going to change anyway. So ignore the details—for a while. Nail the basics first and worry about the specifics later.

When we start designing something, we sketch out ideas with a big, thick Sharpie marker, instead of a ballpoint pen. Why? Pen points are too fine. They're too high-resolution. They encourage you to worry about things that you shouldn't worry about yet, like perfecting the shading or whether to use a dotted or dashed line. You end up focusing on things that should still be out of focus.

A Sharpie makes it impossible to drill down that deep. You can only draw shapes, lines, and boxes. That's good. The big picture is all you should be worrying about in the beginning.

Walt Stanchfield, famed drawing instructor for Walt

Disney Studios, used to encourage animators to "forget the detail" at first. The reason: Detail just doesn't buy you anything in the early stages.*

Besides, you often can't recognize the details that matter most until *after* you start building. That's when you see what needs more attention. You feel what's missing. And that's when you need to pay attention, not sooner.

---

*Walt Stanchfield, *Drawn to Life: 20 Golden Years of Disney Master Classes,* vol. 1, *The Walt Stanchfield Lectures,* Oxford, UK: Focal Press, 2009.

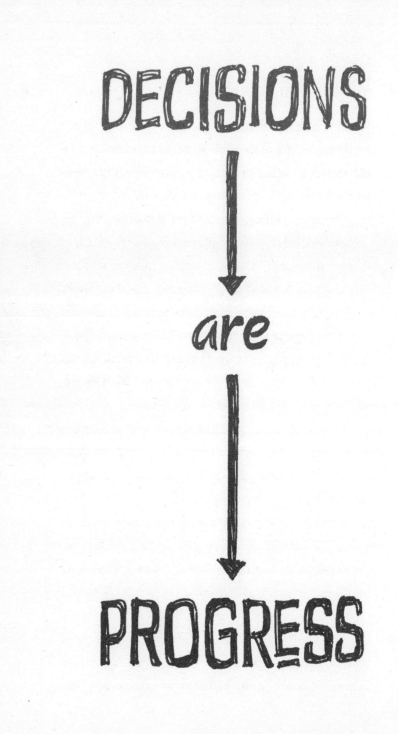

Making the call is making progress

When you put off decisions, they pile up. And piles end up ignored, dealt with in haste, or thrown out. As a result, the individual problems in those piles stay unresolved.

Whenever you can, swap "Let's think about it" for "Let's decide on it." Commit to making decisions. Don't wait for the perfect solution. Decide and move forward.

You want to get into the rhythm of making choices. When you get in that flow of making decision after decision, you build momentum and boost morale. Decisions are progress. Each one you make is a brick in your foundation. You can't build on top of "We'll decide later," but you *can* build on top of "Done."

The problem comes when you postpone decisions in the hope that a perfect answer will come to you later. It won't. You're as likely to make a great call today as you are tomorrow.

An example from our world: For a long time, we avoided creating an affiliate program for our products because the "perfect" solution seemed way too complicated: We'd have to automate payments, mail out checks, figure out foreign tax laws for overseas affiliates, etc. The breakthrough came when we asked, "What can we easily do right now that's good enough?" The answer: Pay affiliates in credit instead of cash. So that's what we did.

We stuck with that approach for a while and then eventually implemented a system that pays cash. And that's a big part of this: You don't have to live with a decision forever. If you make a mistake, you can correct it later.

It doesn't matter how much you plan, you'll still get some stuff wrong anyway. Don't make things worse by overanalyzing and delaying before you even get going.

Long projects zap morale. The longer it takes to develop, the less likely it is to launch. Make the call, make progress, and get something out now—while you've got the motivation and momentum to do so.

Be a curator

You don't make a great museum by putting all the art in the world into a single room. That's a warehouse. What makes a museum great is the stuff that's *not* on the walls. Someone says no. A curator is involved, making conscious decisions about what should stay and what should go. There's an editing process. There's a lot more stuff *off* the walls than *on* the walls. The best is a sub-sub-subset of all the possibilities.

It's the stuff you leave out that matters. So constantly look for things to remove, simplify, and streamline. Be a curator. Stick to what's truly essential. Pare things down until you're left with only the most important stuff. Then do it again. You can always add stuff back in later if you need to.

Zingerman's is one of America's best-known delis. And it got that way because its owners think of themselves as curators. They're not just filling their shelves. They're *curating* them.

There's a reason for every olive oil the team at Zingerman's sells: They believe each one is great. Usually, they've known the supplier for years. They've visited and picked olives with them. That's why they can vouch for each oil's authentic, full-bodied flavor.

For example, look how the owner of Zingerman's describes Pasolivo Olive Oil on the company Web site:

I tasted this oil for the first time years ago, on a random recommendation and sample. There are plenty of oils that come in nice bottles with very endearing stories to tell—this was no exception— but most simply aren't that great. By contrast Pasolivo got my attention as soon as I tasted it. It's powerful, full and fruity. Everything I like in an oil, without any drawbacks. It still stands as one of America's best oils, on par with the great rustic oils of Tuscany. Strongly recommended.*

The owner actually tried the oil and chooses to carry it based on its taste. It's not about packaging, marketing, or price. It's about quality. He tried it and knew his store had to carry it. That's the approach you should take too.

---

*Pasolivo Olive Oil, Zingerman's,
www.zingermans.com/product.aspx?productid=o-psl

Throw less at the problem

Watch chef Gordon Ramsay's *Kitchen Nightmares* and you'll see a pattern. The menus at failing restaurants offer too many dishes. The owners think making every dish under the sun will broaden the appeal of the restaurant. Instead it makes for crappy food (and creates inventory headaches).

That's why Ramsay's first step is nearly always to trim the menu, usually from thirty-plus dishes to around ten. Think about that. Improving the current menu doesn't come first. Trimming it down comes first. Then he polishes what's left.

When things aren't working, the natural inclination is to throw more at the problem. More people, time, and money. All that ends up doing is making the problem bigger. The right way to go is the opposite direction: Cut back.

So do less. Your project won't suffer nearly as much as you fear. In fact, there's a good chance it'll end up even better. You'll be forced to make tough calls and sort out what truly matters.

If you start pushing back deadlines and increasing your budget, you'll never stop.

Focus on what won't change

A lot of companies focus on the next big thing. They latch on to what's hot and new. They follow the latest trends and technology.

That's a fool's path. You start focusing on fashion instead of substance. You start paying attention to things that are constantly changing instead of things that last.

The core of your business should be built around things that won't change. Things that people are going to want today *and* ten years from now. Those are the things you should invest in.

Amazon.com focuses on fast (or free) shipping, great selection, friendly return policies, and affordable prices. These things will always be in high demand.

Japanese automakers also focus on core principles that don't change: reliability, affordability, and practicality. People wanted those things thirty years ago, they want them today, and they'll want them thirty years from now.

For 37signals, things like speed, simplicity, ease of use, and clarity are our focus. Those are timeless desires. People aren't going to wake up in ten years and say, "Man, I wish software was harder to use." They won't say, "I wish this application was slower."

Remember, fashion fades away. When you focus on *permanent* features, you're in bed with things that never go out of style.

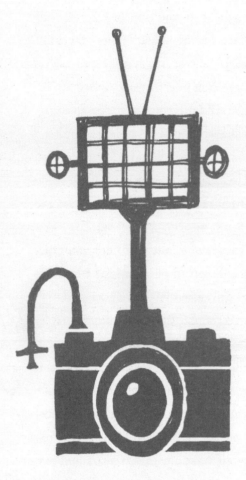

GEAR *doesn't* MATTER

Tone is in your fingers

Guitar gurus say, "Tone is in your fingers." You can buy the same guitar, effects pedals, and amplifier that Eddie Van Halen uses. But when you play that rig, it's still going to sound like you.

Likewise, Eddie could plug into a crappy Strat/Pignose setup at a pawn shop, and you'd still be able to recognize that it's Eddie Van Halen playing. Fancy gear can help, but the truth is your tone comes from you.

It's tempting for people to obsess over tools instead of what they're going to do with those tools. You know the type: Designers who use an avalanche of funky typefaces and fancy Photoshop filters but don't have anything to say. Amateur photographers who want to debate film versus digital endlessly instead of focusing on what actually makes a photograph great.

Many amateur golfers think they need expensive clubs. But it's the swing that matters, not the club. Give Tiger Woods a set of cheap clubs and he'll still destroy you.

People use equipment as a crutch. They don't want to put in the hours on the driving range so they spend a ton in the pro shop. They're looking for a shortcut. But you just don't need the best gear in the world to be good. And you definitely don't need it to get started.

In business, too many people obsess over tools, software tricks, scaling issues, fancy office space, lavish furniture, and other frivolities instead of what really matters. And what really matters is how to actually get customers and make money.

You also see it in people who want to blog, podcast, or shoot videos for their business but get hung up on which tools to use. The content is what matters. You can spend tons on fancy equipment, but if you've got nothing to say . . . well, you've got nothing to say.

Use whatever you've got already or can afford cheaply. Then go. It's not the gear that matters. It's playing what you've got as well as you can. Your tone is in your fingers.

Sell your by-products

When you make something, you always make something else. You can't make just one thing. Everything has a by-product. Observant and creative business minds spot these by-products and see opportunities.

The lumber industry sells what used to be waste—sawdust, chips, and shredded wood—for a pretty profit. You'll find these by-products in synthetic fireplace logs, concrete, ice strengtheners, mulch, particleboard, fuel, and more.

But you're probably not manufacturing anything. That can make it tough to spot your by-products. People at a lumber company see their waste. They can't ignore sawdust. But you don't see yours. Maybe you don't even think you produce any by-products. But that's myopic.

Our last book, *Getting Real,* was a by-product. We wrote that book without even knowing it. The experience that came from building a company and building software was the waste from actually doing the work. We swept up that knowledge first into blog posts, then into a workshop series, then into a .pdf, and then into a paperback. That by-product has made 37signals more than $1 million directly and probably more than another $1 million indirectly. The book you're reading right now is a by-product too.

The rock band Wilco found a valuable by-product in its recording process. The band filmed the creation of an album and released it as a documentary called *I Am Trying to Break Your Heart*. It offered an uncensored and fascinating look at the group's creative process and in-fighting. The band made money off the movie and also used it as a stepping-stone toward reaching a wider audience.

Henry Ford learned of a process for turning wood scraps from the production of Model T's into charcoal briquets. He built a charcoal plant and Ford Charcoal was created (later renamed Kingsford Charcoal). Today, Kingsford is still the leading manufacturer of charcoal in America.*

Software companies don't usually think about writing books. Bands don't usually think about filming the recording process. Car manufacturers don't usually think about selling charcoal. There's probably something you haven't thought about that you could sell too.

---

*"About Kingsford: Simply a Matter of Taste," Kingsford, www.kingsford.com/about/index.htm

GET
IT OUT
THERE!

Launch now

When is your product or service finished? When should you put it out on the market? When is it safe to let people have it? Probably a lot sooner than you're comfortable with. Once your product does what it needs to do, get it out there.

Just because you've still got a list of things to do doesn't mean it's not done. Don't hold everything else up because of a few leftovers. You can do them later. And doing them later may mean doing them better, too.

Think about it this way: If you had to launch your business in two weeks, what would you cut out? Funny how a question like that forces you to focus. You suddenly realize there's a lot of stuff you don't need. And what you *do* need seems obvious. When you impose a deadline, you gain clarity. It's the best way to get to that gut instinct that tells you, "We don't need this."

Put off anything you don't need for launch. Build the necessities now, worry about the luxuries later. If you really think about it, there's a whole lot you don't need on day one.

When we launched Basecamp, we didn't even have the ability to bill customers! Because the product billed in monthly cycles, we knew we had a thirty-day gap to figure it out. So we used the time before launch to solve more urgent problems that actually mattered on day one. Day 30 could wait.

Camper, a brand of shoes, opened a store in San Francisco before construction was even finished and called it a Walk in Progress. Customers could draw on the walls of the empty store. Camper displayed shoes on cheap plywood laid over dozens of shoe boxes. The most popular message written by customers on the walls: "Keep the store just the way it is."*

Likewise, the founders of Crate and Barrel didn't wait to build fancy displays when they opened their first store. They turned over the crates and barrels that the merchandise came in and stacked products on top of them.†

Don't mistake this approach for skimping on quality, either. You still want to make something great. This approach just recognizes that the best way to get there is through iterations. Stop imagining what's going to work. Find out for real.

---

*Fara Warner, "Walk in Progress," *Fast Company,* Dec. 19, 2007, www.fastcompany.com/magazine/58/lookfeel.html
†Matt Valley, "The Crate and Barrel Story," *Retail Traffic,* June 1, 2001, retailtrafficmag.com/mag/retail_crate_barrel_story

CHAPTER

PRODUCTIVITY

Illusions of agreement

The business world is littered with dead documents that do nothing but waste people's time. Reports no one reads, diagrams no one looks at, and specs that never resemble the finished product. These things take forever to make but only seconds to forget.

If you need to explain something, try getting real with it. Instead of describing what something looks like, draw it. Instead of explaining what something sounds like, hum it. Do everything you can to remove layers of abstraction.

The problem with abstractions (like reports and documents) is that they create illusions of agreement. A hundred people can read the same words, but in their heads, they're imagining a hundred different things.

That's why you want to get to something real right away. That's when you get true understanding. It's like when we read about characters in a book—we each picture them differently in our heads. But when we actually *see* people, we all know exactly what they look like.

When the team at Alaska Airlines wanted to build a new Airport of the Future, they didn't rely on blueprints and sketches. They got a warehouse and built mock-ups using cardboard boxes for podiums, kiosks, and belts. The team then built a small prototype in

Anchorage to test systems with real passengers and employees. The design that resulted from this getting-real process has significantly reduced wait times and increased agent productivity.*

Widely admired furniture craftsman Sam Maloof felt it was impossible to make a working drawing to show all the intricate and fine details that go into a chair or stool. "Many times I do not know how a certain area is to be done until I start working with a chisel, rasp, or whatever tool is needed for that particular job," he said.†

That's the path we all should take. Get the chisel out and start making something real. Anything else is just a distraction.

---

*Dave Demerjian, "Hustle & Flow," *Fast Company*,
www.fastcompany.com/magazine/123/hustle-and-flow.html
†"Maloof on Maloof: Quotations and Works of Sam Maloof,"
Smithsonian American Art Museum,
americanart.si.edu/exhibitions/online/maloof/introduction

Reasons to quit

It's easy to put your head down and just work on what you *think* needs to be done. It's a lot harder to pull your head up and ask why. Here are some important questions to ask yourself to ensure you're doing work that matters:

Why are you doing this? Ever find yourself working on something without knowing exactly why? Someone just told you to do it. It's pretty common, actually. That's why it's important to ask why you're working on _____ . What is this for? Who benefits? What's the motivation behind it? Knowing the answers to these questions will help you better understand the work itself.

What problem are you solving? What's the problem? Are customers confused? Are you confused? Is something not clear enough? Was something not possible before that should be possible now? Sometimes when you ask these questions, you'll find you're solving an *imaginary* problem. That's when it's time to stop and reevaluate what the hell you're doing.

Is this actually useful? Are you making something useful or just making something? It's easy to confuse enthusiasm with usefulness. Sometimes it's fine to play a bit and build something cool. But eventually you've got to stop and ask yourself if it's useful, too. Cool wears off. Useful never does.

Are you adding value? Adding something is easy; adding *value* is hard. Is this thing you're working on actually making your product more valuable for customers? Can they get more out of it than they did before? Sometimes things you think are adding value actually subtract from it. Too much ketchup can ruin the fries. Value is about balance.

Will this change behavior? Is what you're working on really going to change anything? Don't add something unless it has a real impact on how people use your product.

Is there an easier way? Whenever you're working on something, ask, "Is there an easier way?" You'll often find this easy way is more than good enough for now. Problems are usually pretty simple. We just imagine that they require hard solutions.

What could you be doing instead? What can't you do because you're doing this? This is especially important for small teams with constrained resources.

That's when prioritization is even more important. If you work on A, can you still do B and C before April? If not, would you rather have B and C instead of A? If you're stuck on something for a long period of time, that means there are other things you're not getting done.

Is it really worth it? Is what you're doing really worth it? Is this meeting worth pulling six people off their work for an hour? Is it worth pulling an all-nighter tonight, or could you just finish it up tomorrow? Is it worth getting all stressed out over a press release from a competitor? Is it worth spending your money on advertising? Determine the real value of what you're about to do before taking the plunge.

Keep asking yourself (and others) the questions listed above. You don't need to make it a formal process, but don't let it slide, either.

Also, don't be timid about your conclusions. Sometimes abandoning what you're working on is the right move, even if you've already put in a lot of effort. Don't throw good time after bad work.

PRODU CTIVITY

INTERRUPTION

Interruption is the enemy of productivity

If you're constantly staying late and working weekends, it's not because there's too much work to be done. It's because you're not getting enough done at work. And the reason is interruptions.

Think about it: When do you get most of your work done? If you're like most people, it's at night or early in the morning. It's no coincidence that these are the times when nobody else is around.

At 2 p.m., people are usually in a meeting or answering e-mail or chatting with colleagues. Those taps on the shoulder and little impromptu get-togethers may seem harmless, but they're actually corrosive to productivity. Interruption is not collaboration, it's just interruption. And when you're interrupted, you're not getting work done.

Interruptions break your workday into a series of work moments. Forty-five minutes and then you have a call. Fifteen minutes and then you have lunch. An hour later, you have an afternoon meeting. Before you know it, it's five o'clock, and you've only had a couple uninterrupted hours to get your work done. You can't get meaningful things done when you're constantly going start, stop, start, stop.

Instead, you should get in the alone zone. Long stretches of alone time are when you're most productive. When you don't have to mind-shift between various tasks, you get a boatload done. (Ever notice how much work you get done on a plane since you're offline and there are zero outside distractions?)

Getting into that zone takes time and requires avoiding interruptions. It's like REM sleep: You don't just go directly into REM sleep. You go to sleep first and then make your way to REM. Any interruptions force you to start over. And just as REM is when the real sleep magic happens, the alone zone is where the real productivity magic happens.

Your alone zone doesn't have to be in the wee hours, though. You can set up a rule at work that half the day is set aside for alone time. Decree that from 10 a.m. to 2 p.m., people can't talk to each other (except during lunch). Or make the first or last half of the day *your* alone-time period. Or instead of casual Fridays, try no-talk Thursdays. Just make sure this period is unbroken in order to avoid productivity-zapping interruptions.

And go all the way with it. A successful alone-time period means letting go of communication addiction. During alone time, give up instant messages, phone calls, e-mail, and meetings. Just shut up and get to work. You'll be surprised how much more you get done.

Also, when you do collaborate, try to use passive communication tools, like e-mail, that don't require an instant reply, instead of interruptive ones, like phone calls and face-to-face meetings. That way people can respond when it's convenient for them, instead of being forced to drop everything right away.

Your day is under siege by interruptions. It's on you to fight back.

Meetings are toxic

The worst interruptions of all are meetings. Here's why:

- They're usually about words and abstract concepts, not real things.
- They usually convey an abysmally small amount of information per minute.
- They drift off-subject easier than a Chicago cab in a snowstorm.
- They require thorough preparation that most people don't have time for.
- They frequently have agendas so vague that nobody is really sure of the goal.
- They often include at least one moron who inevitably gets his turn to waste everyone's time with nonsense.
- Meetings procreate. One meeting leads to another meeting leads to another . . .

It's also unfortunate that meetings are typically scheduled like TV shows. You set aside thirty minutes or an hour because that's how scheduling software works (you'll never see anyone schedule a seven-minute meeting with Outlook). Too bad. If it only takes seven minutes to accomplish a meeting's goal, then that's all the time you should spend. Don't stretch seven into thirty.

When you think about it, the true cost of meetings is staggering. Let's say you're going to schedule a meeting that lasts one hour, and you invite ten people to attend. That's actually a ten-hour meeting, not a one-hour meeting. You're trading ten hours of productivity for one hour of meeting time. And it's probably more like fifteen hours, because there are mental switching costs that come with stopping what you're doing, going somewhere else to meet, and then resuming what you were doing beforehand.

Is it ever OK to trade ten or fifteen hours of productivity for one hour of meeting? Sometimes, maybe. But that's a pretty hefty price to pay. Judged on a pure cost basis, meetings of this size quickly become liabilities, not assets. Think about the time you're actually losing and ask yourself if it's really worth it.

If you decide you absolutely *must* get together, try to make your meeting a productive one by sticking to these simple rules:

- Set a timer. When it rings, meeting's over. Period.
- Invite as few people as possible.
- Always have a clear agenda.
- Begin with a specific problem.

- Meet at the site of the problem instead of a conference room. Point to real things and suggest real changes.
- End with a solution and make someone responsible for implementing it.

Good enough is fine

A lot of people get off on solving problems with complicated solutions. Flexing your intellectual muscles can be
intoxicating. Then you start looking for another big
challenge that gives you that same rush, regardless of
whether it's a good idea or not.

A better idea: Find a judo solution, one that delivers maximum efficiency with minimum effort. Judo
solutions are all about getting the most out of doing
the least. Whenever you face an obstacle, look for a
way to judo it.

Part of this is recognizing that problems are nego-
tiable. Let's say your challenge is to get a bird's-eye view.
One way to do it is to climb Mount Everest. That's the
ambitious solution. But then again, you could take an
elevator to the top of a tall building. That's a judo
solution.

Problems can usually be solved with simple, mun-
dane solutions. That means there's no glamorous work.
You don't get to show off your amazing skills. You just
build something that gets the job done and then move
on. This approach may not earn you oohs and aahs, but
it lets you get on with it.

Look at political campaign ads. A big issue pops up,
and politicians have an ad about it on the air the next

day. The production quality is low. They use photos instead of live footage. They have static, plain-text headlines instead of fancy animated graphics. The only audio is a voice-over done by an unseen narrator. Despite all that, the ad is still good enough. If they waited weeks to perfect it, it would come out too late. It's a situation where timeliness is more important than polish or even quality.

When good enough gets the job done, go for it. It's way better than wasting resources or, even worse, doing nothing because you can't afford the complex solution. And remember, you can usually turn good enough into great later.

QUICK WINS

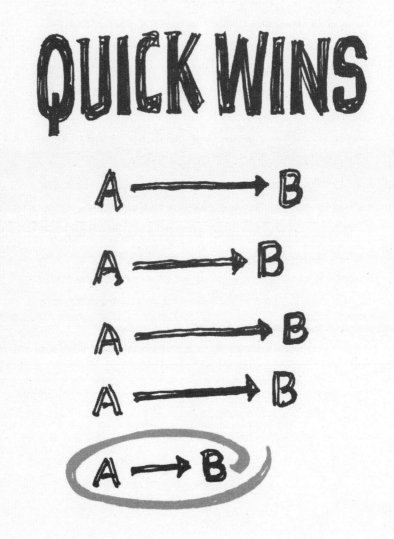

Quick wins

Momentum fuels motivation. It keeps you going. It drives you. Without it, you can't go anywhere. If you aren't motivated by what you're working on, it won't be very good.

The way you build momentum is by getting something done and then moving on to the next thing. No one likes to be stuck on an endless project with no finish line in sight. Being in the trenches for nine months and not having anything to show for it is a real buzzkill. Eventually it just burns you out. To keep your momentum and motivation up, get in the habit of accomplishing small victories along the way. Even a tiny improvement can give you a good jolt of momentum.

The longer something takes, the less likely it is that you're going to finish it.

Excitement comes from doing something and then letting customers have at it. Planning a menu for a year is boring. Getting the new menu out, serving the food, and getting feedback is exciting. So don't wait too long—you'll smother your sparks if you do.

If you absolutely have to work on long-term projects, try to dedicate one day a week (or every two weeks) to small victories that generate enthusiasm. Small victories let you celebrate and release good news. And you want a steady stream of good news. When there's something new to announce every two weeks, you energize your team and give your customers something to be excited about.

So ask yourself, "What can we do in two weeks?" And then do it. Get it out there and let people use it, taste it, play it, or whatever. The quicker it's in the hands of customers, the better off you'll be.

Don't be a hero

A lot of times it's better to be a quitter than a hero.

For example, let's say you think a task can be done in two hours. But four hours into it, you're still only a quarter of the way done. The natural instinct is to think, "But I can't give up now, I've already spent four hours on this!"

So you go into hero mode. You're determined to make it work (and slightly embarrassed that it isn't already working). You grab your cape and shut yourself off from the world.

And sometimes that kind of sheer effort overload works. But is it worth it? Probably not. The task was worth it when you thought it would cost two hours, not sixteen. In those sixteen hours, you could have gotten a bunch of other things done. Plus, you cut yourself off from feedback, which can lead you even further down the wrong path. Even heroes need a fresh pair of eyes sometimes—someone else to give them a reality check.

We've experienced this problem firsthand. So we decided that if anything takes one of us longer than two weeks, we've got to bring other people in to take a look. They might not do any work on the task, but at least they can review it quickly and give their two cents. Sometimes an obvious solution is staring you right in the face, but you can't even see it.

Keep in mind that the obvious solution might very well be quitting. People automatically associate quitting with failure, but sometimes that's *exactly* what you should do. If you already spent too much time on something that wasn't worth it, walk away. You can't get that time back. The worst thing you can do now is waste even more time.

Go to sleep

Forgoing sleep is a bad idea. Sure, you get those extra hours right now, but you pay in spades later: You destroy your creativity, morale, and attitude.

Once in a while, you can pull an all-nighter if you fully understand the consequences. Just don't make it a habit. If it becomes a constant, the costs start to mount:

Stubbornness: When you're really tired, it always seems easier to plow down whatever bad path you happen to be on instead of reconsidering the route. The finish line is a constant mirage and you wind up walking in the desert way too long.

Lack of creativity: Creativity is one of the first things to go when you lose sleep. What distinguishes people who are ten times more effective than the norm is not that they work ten times as hard; it's that they use their creativity to come up with solutions that require one-tenth of the effort. Without sleep, you stop coming up with those one-tenth solutions.

Diminished morale: When your brain isn't firing on all cylinders, it loves to feed on less demanding tasks. Like reading yet another article about stuff that doesn't matter. When you're tired, you lose motivation to attack the big problems.

Irritability: Your ability to remain patient and tolerant is severely reduced when you're tired. If you encounter someone who's acting like a fool, there's a good chance that person is suffering from sleep deprivation.

These are just some of the costs you incur when not getting enough sleep. Yet some people still develop a masochistic sense of honor about sleep deprivation. They even brag about how tired they are. Don't be impressed. It'll come back to bite them in the ass.

Your estimates suck

We're all terrible estimators. We think we can guess how long something will take, when we really have no idea. We see everything going according to a best-case scenario, without the delays that inevitably pop up. Reality never sticks to best-case scenarios.

That's why estimates that stretch weeks, months, and years into the future are fantasies. The truth is you just don't know what's going to happen that far in advance.

How often do you think a quick trip to the grocery store will take only a few minutes and then it winds up taking an hour? And remember when cleaning out the attic took you all day instead of just the couple of hours you thought it would? Or sometimes it's the opposite, like that time you planned on spending four hours raking the yard only to have it take just thirty-five minutes. We humans are just plain *bad* at estimating.

Even with these simple tasks, our estimates are often off by a factor of two or more. If we can't be accurate when estimating a few hours, how can we expect to accurately predict the length of a "six-month project"?

Plus, we're not just a little bit wrong when we guess how long something will take—we're a lot wrong. That means if you're guessing six months, you might be *way* off: We're not talking seven months instead of six, we're talking one year instead of six months.

That's why Boston's "Big Dig" highway project finished five years late and billions over budget. Or the Denver International Airport opened sixteen months late, at a cost overrun of $2 billion.

The solution: Break the big thing into smaller things. The smaller it is, the easier it is to estimate. You're probably still going to get it wrong, but you'll be a lot less wrong than if you estimated a big project. If something takes twice as long as you expected, better to have it be a small project that's a couple *weeks* over rather than a long one that's a couple *months* over.

Keep breaking your time frames down into smaller chunks. Instead of one twelve-week project, structure it as twelve one-week projects. Instead of guesstimating at tasks that take thirty hours or more, break them down into more realistic six-to-ten-hour chunks. Then go one step at a time.

LONG LISTS *don't* GET DONE

TASKS

Long lists don't get done

Start making smaller to-do lists too. Long lists collect dust. When's the last time you finished a long list of things? You might have knocked off the first few, but chances are you eventually abandoned it (or blindly checked off items that weren't really done properly).

Long lists are guilt trips. The longer the list of unfinished items, the worse you feel about it. And at a certain point, you just stop looking at it because it makes you feel bad. Then you stress out and the whole thing turns into a big mess.

There's a better way. Break that long list down into a bunch of smaller lists. For example, break a single list of a hundred items into ten lists of ten items. That means when you finish an item on a list, you've completed 10 percent of that list, instead of 1 percent.

Yes, you still have the same amount of stuff left to do. But now you can look at the small picture and find satisfaction, motivation, and progress. That's a lot better than staring at the huge picture and being terrified and demoralized.

Whenever you can, divide problems into smaller and smaller pieces until you're able to deal with them completely and quickly. Simply rearranging your tasks this way can have an amazing impact on your productivity and motivation.

And a quick suggestion about prioritization: Don't prioritize with numbers or labels. Avoid saying, "This is high priority, this is low priority." Likewise, don't say, "This is a three, this is a two, this is a one, this is a three," etc. Do that and you'll almost always end up with a ton of really high-priority things. That's not really prioritizing.

Instead, prioritize visually. Put the most important thing at the top. When you're done with that, the next thing on the list becomes the next most important thing. That way you'll only have a single next most important thing to do at a time. And that's enough.

MAKE

BIG   TINY

DECISIONS

Make tiny decisions

Big decisions are hard to make and hard to change. And once you make one, the tendency is to continue believing you made the right decision, even if you didn't. You stop being objective.

Once ego and pride are on the line, you can't change your mind without looking bad. The desire to save face trumps the desire to make the right call. And then there's inertia too: The more steam you put into going in one direction, the harder it is to change course.

Instead, make choices that are small enough that they're effectively temporary. When you make tiny decisions, you can't make big mistakes. These small decisions mean you can afford to change. There's no big penalty if you mess up. You just fix it.

Making tiny decisions doesn't mean you can't make big plans or think big ideas. It just means you believe the best way to achieve those big things is one tiny decision at a time.

Polar explorer Ben Saunders said that during his solo North Pole expedition (thirty-one marathons back-to-back, seventy-two days alone) the "huge decision" was often so horrifically overwhelming to contemplate that his day-to-day decision making rarely extended beyond "getting to that bit of ice a few yards in front of me."

Attainable goals like that are the best ones to have. Ones you can actually accomplish and build on. You get to say, "We nailed it. Done!" Then you get going on the next one. That's a lot more satisfying than some pie-in-the-sky fantasy goal you never meet.

CHAPTER

COMPETITORS

Don't copy

Sometimes copying can be part of the learning process, like when you see an art student replicating a painting in a museum or a drummer playing along to John Bonham's solo on Led Zeppelin's "Moby Dick." When you're a student, this sort of imitation can be a helpful tool on the path to discovering your own voice.

Unfortunately, copying in the business arena is usually more nefarious. Maybe it's because of the copy-and-paste world we live in these days. You can steal someone's words, images, or code instantly. And that means it's tempting to try to build a business by being a copycat.

That's a formula for failure, though. The problem with this sort of copying is it skips understanding—and understanding is how you grow. You have to understand why something works or why something is the way it is. When you just copy and paste, you miss that. You just repurpose the last layer instead of understanding all the layers underneath.

So much of the work an original creator puts into something is invisible. It's buried beneath the surface. The copycat doesn't really know why something looks the way it looks or feels the way it feels or reads the way it reads. The copy is a faux finish. It delivers no substance, no understanding, and nothing to base future decisions on.

Plus, if you're a copycat, you can never keep up. You're always in a passive position. You never lead; you always follow. You give birth to something that's already behind the times—just a knockoff, an inferior version of the original. That's no way to live.

How do you know if you're copying someone? If someone else is doing the bulk of the work, you're copying. Be influenced, but don't steal.

Decommoditize your product

If you're successful, people will try to copy what you do. It's just a fact of life. But there's a great way to protect yourself from copycats: Make *you* part of your product or service. Inject what's unique about the way you think into what you sell. Decommoditize your product. Make it something no one else can offer.

Look at Zappos.com, a billion-dollar online shoe retailer. A pair of sneakers from Zappos is the same as a pair from Foot Locker or any other retailer. But Zappos sets itself apart by injecting CEO Tony Hsieh's obsession with customer service into everything it does.

At Zappos, customer-service employees don't use scripts and are allowed to talk at length with customers. The call center and the company's headquarters are in the same place, not oceans apart. And all Zappos employees—even those who don't work in customer service or fulfillment—start out by spending four weeks answering phones and working in the warehouse. It's this devotion to customer service that makes Zappos unique among shoe sellers.*

Another example is Polyface, an environmentally

---

*"A Shine on Their Shoes," *BusinessWeek*, Dec. 5, 2005, www.business week.com/magazine/content/05_49/b3962118.htm

friendly Virginia farm owned by Joel Salatin. Salatin has a strong set of beliefs and runs his business accordingly. Polyface sells the idea that it does things a bigger agribusiness can't do. Even though it's more expensive to do so, it feeds cows grass instead of corn and never gives them antibiotics. It never ships food. Anyone is welcome to visit the farm anytime and go anywhere (try that at a typical meat-processing plant). Polyface doesn't just sell chickens, it sells a way of thinking. And customers love Polyface for it. Some customers routinely drive from 150 miles away to get "clean" meat for their families.*

Pour yourself into your product and everything *around* your product too: how you sell it, how you support it, how you explain it, and how you deliver it. Competitors can never copy the *you* in your product.

---

*"The Polyface Story," www.polyfacefarms.com/story.aspx

Pick a fight

If you think a competitor sucks, say so. When you do that, you'll find that others who agree with you will rally to your side. Being the anti-_____ is a great way to differentiate yourself and attract followers.

For example, Dunkin' Donuts likes to position itself as the anti-Starbucks. Its ads mock Starbucks for using "Fritalian" terms instead of small, medium, and large. Another Dunkin' campaign is centered on a taste test in which it beat Starbucks. There's even a site called DunkinBeatStarbucks.com where visitors can send e-cards with statements like "Friends don't let friends drink Starbucks."

Audi is another example. It's been taking on the old guard of car manufacturers. It puts "old luxury" brands like Rolls-Royce and Mercedes "on notice" in ads touting Audi as the fresh luxury alternative. Audi takes on Lexus's automatic parking systems with ads that say Audi drivers know how to park their own cars. Another ad gives a side-by-side comparison of BMW and Audi owners: The BMW owner uses the rearview mirror to adjust his hair while the Audi driver uses the mirror to see what's behind him.

Apple jabs at Microsoft with ads that compare Mac and PC owners, and 7UP bills itself as the Uncola.

Under Armour positions itself as Nike for a new generation.

All these examples show the power and direction you can gain by having a target in your sights. Who do you want to take a shot at?

You can even pit yourself as the opponent of an entire industry. Dyson's Airblade starts with the premise that the hand-dryer industry is a failure and then sells itself as faster and more hygienic than the others. I Can't Believe It's Not Butter puts its enemy right there in its product name.

Having an enemy gives you a great story to tell customers, too. Taking a stand always stands out. People get stoked by conflict. They take sides. Passions are ignited. And that's a good way to get people to take notice.

UNDERDO *your* COMPETITION

Underdo your competition

Conventional wisdom says that to beat your competitors, you need to one-up them. If they have four features, you need five (or fifteen, or twenty-five). If they're
spending $20,000, you need to spend $30,000. If they
have fifty employees, you need a hundred.

This sort of one-upping, Cold War mentality is a
dead end. When you get suckered into an arms race,
you wind up in a never-ending battle that costs you
massive amounts of money, time, and drive. And it
forces you to constantly be on the defensive, too. Defensive companies can't think ahead; they can only think
behind. They don't lead; they follow.

So what do you do instead? Do less than your competitors to beat them. Solve the simple problems and
leave the hairy, difficult, nasty problems to the competition. Instead of one-upping, try one-downing. Instead
of outdoing, try underdoing.

The bicycle world provides a great example. For
years, major bicycle brands focused on the latest in high-
tech equipment: mountain bikes with suspension and
ultrastrong disc brakes, or lightweight titanium road
bikes with carbon-fiber everything. And it was assumed
that bikes should have multiple gears: three, ten, or
twenty-one.

But recently, fixed-gear bicycles have boomed in popularity, despite being as low-tech as you can get. These bikes have just one gear. Some models don't have brakes. The advantage: They're simpler, lighter, cheaper, and don't require as much maintenance.

Another great example of a product that is succeeding by underdoing the competition: the Flip—an ultrasimple, point-and-shoot, compact camcorder that's taken a significant percentage of the market in a short time. Look at all the things the Flip does *not* deliver:

- No big screen (and the tiny screen doesn't swing out for self-portraits either)
- No photo-taking ability
- No tapes or discs (you have to offload the videos to a computer)
- No menus
- No settings
- No video light
- No viewfinder
- No special effects
- No headphone jack
- No lens cap
- No memory card
- No optical zoom

The Flip wins fans because it only does a few simple things and it does them well. It's easy and fun to use. It goes places a bigger camera would never go and gets used by people who would never use a fancier camera.

Don't shy away from the fact that your product or service does less. Highlight it. Be proud of it. Sell it as aggressively as competitors sell their extensive feature lists.

Who cares what they're doing?

In the end, it's not worth paying much attention to the competition anyway. Why not? Because worrying about the competition quickly turns into an obsession. What are they doing right now? Where are they going next? How should we react?

Every little move becomes something to be analyzed. And that's a terrible mind-set. It leads to overwhelming stress and anxiety. That state of mind is bad soil for growing anything.

It's a pointless exercise anyway. The competitive landscape changes all the time. Your competitor tomorrow may be completely different from your competitor today. It's out of your control. What's the point of worrying about things you can't control?

Focus on yourself instead. What's going on in here is way more important than what's going on out there. When you spend time worrying about someone else, you can't spend that time improving yourself.

Focus on competitors too much and you wind up diluting your own vision. Your chances of coming up with something fresh go way down when you keep feeding your brain other people's ideas. You become reactionary instead of visionary. You wind up offering your competitor's products with a different coat of paint.

If you're planning to build "the iPod killer" or "the next Pokemon," you're already dead. You're allowing the competition to set the parameters. You're not going to out-Apple Apple. They're defining the rules of the game. And you can't beat someone who's making the rules. You need to redefine the rules, not just build something slightly better.

Don't ask yourself whether you're "beating" Apple (or whoever the big boy is in your industry). That's the wrong question to ask. It's not a win-or-lose battle. Their profits and costs are theirs. Yours are yours.

If you're just going to be like everyone else, why are you even doing this? If you merely replicate competitors, there's no point to your existence. Even if you wind up losing, it's better to go down fighting for what you believe in instead of just imitating others.

CHAPTER

EVOLUTION

Say no by default

If I'd listened to customers,
I'd have given them a faster horse.
—HENRY FORD

It's so easy to say yes. Yes to another feature, yes to an overly optimistic deadline, yes to a mediocre design. Soon, the stack of things you've said yes to grows so tall you can't even see the things you should really be doing.

Start getting into the habit of saying no—even to many of your best ideas. Use the power of no to get your priorities straight. You rarely regret saying no. But you often wind up regretting saying yes.

People avoid saying no because confrontation makes them uncomfortable. But the alternative is even worse. You drag things out, make things complicated, and work on ideas you don't believe in.

It's like a relationship: Breaking one up is hard to do, but staying in it just because you're too chicken to drop the ax is even worse. Deal with the brief discomfort of confrontation up front and avoid the long-term regret.

Don't believe that "customer is always right" stuff, either. Let's say you're a chef. If enough of your customers say your food is too salty or too hot, you change it. But if a few persnickety patrons tell you to add bananas to your lasagna, you're going to turn them down, and that's OK. Making a few vocal customers happy isn't worth it if it ruins the product for everyone else.

ING Direct has built the fastest-growing bank in America by saying no. When customers ask for a credit card, the answer is no. When they ask for an online brokerage, the answer is no. When they ask if they can open an account with a million dollars in it, the answer is no (the bank has a strict deposit maximum). ING wants to keep things simple. That's why the bank offers just a few savings accounts, certificates of deposit, and mutual funds—and that's it.

Don't be a jerk about saying no, though. Just be honest. If you're not willing to yield to a customer request, be polite and explain why. People are surprisingly understanding when you take the time to explain your point of view. You may even win them over to your way of thinking. If not, recommend a competitor if you think there's a better solution out there. It's better to have people be happy using someone else's product than disgruntled using yours.

Your goal is to make sure your product stays right for you. You're the one who has to believe in it most. That way, you can say, "I think you'll love it because I love it."

Let your customers outgrow you

Maybe you've seen this scenario: There's a customer that's paying a company a lot of money. The company tries to please that customer in any way possible. It tweaks and changes the product per this one customer's requests and starts to alienate its general customer base.

Then one day that big customer winds up leaving and the company is left holding the bag—and the bag is a product that's ideally suited to someone who's not there anymore. And now it's a bad fit for everyone else.

When you stick with your current customers come hell or high water, you wind up cutting yourself off from new ones. Your product or service becomes so tailored to your current customers that it stops appealing to fresh blood. And that's how your company starts to die.

After our first product had been around for a while, we started getting some heat from folks who had been with us from the beginning. They said they were starting to grow out of the application. Their businesses were changing and they wanted us to change our product to mirror their newfound complexity and requirements.

We said no. Here's why: We'd rather our customers grow out of our products eventually than never be able to grow into them in the first place. Adding power-user features to satisfy some can intimidate those who aren't on board yet. Scaring away new customers is worse than losing old customers.

When you let customers outgrow you, you'll most likely wind up with a product that's basic—and that's fine. Small, simple, basic needs are constant. There's an endless supply of customers who need exactly that.

And there are always more people who are *not* using your product than people who are. Make sure you make it easy for these people to get on board. That's where your continued growth potential lies.

People and situations change. You can't be everything to everyone. Companies need to be true to a *type* of customer more than a specific individual customer with changing needs.

REVOLUTIONARY!
NEW! HOT!
Amazing! FASTER!

don't confuse ENTHUSIASM
with PRIORITY

Useful.

Don't confuse enthusiasm with priority

Coming up with a great idea gives you a rush. You start imagining the possibilities and the benefits. And of course, you want all that right away. So you drop every-thing else you're working on and begin pursuing your latest, greatest idea.

Bad move. The enthusiasm you have for a new idea is not an accurate indicator of its true worth. What seems like a sure-fire hit right now often gets down-graded to just a "nice to have" by morning. And "nice to have" isn't worth putting everything else on hold.

We have ideas for new features all the time. On top of that, we get dozens of interesting ideas from cus-tomers every day too. Sure, it'd be fun to immediately chase all these ideas to see where they lead. But if we did that, we'd just wind up running on a treadmill and never get anywhere.

So let your latest grand ideas cool off for a while first. By all means, have as many great ideas as you can. Get excited about them. Just don't act in the heat of the moment. Write them down and park them for a few days. Then, evaluate their actual priority with a calm mind.

AT-HOME
GOOD

Be at-home good

You know what it feels like. You go to a store. You're comparing a few different products, and you're sold on the one that sounds like it's the best deal. It's got the most features. It looks the coolest. The packaging looks hot. There's sensational copy on the box. Everything seems great.

But then you get it home, and it doesn't deliver. It's not as easy to use as you thought it'd be. It has too many features you don't need. You end up feeling that you've been taken. You didn't really get what you needed and you realize you spent too much.

You just bought an in-store-good product. That's a product you're more excited about in the store than you are after you've actually used it.

Smart companies make the opposite: something that's at-home good. When you get the product home, you're actually more impressed with it than you were at the store. You live with it and grow to like it more and more. And you tell your friends, too.

When you create an at-home-good product, you may have to sacrifice a bit of in-store sizzle. A product that executes on the basics beautifully may not seem as sexy as competitors loaded with bells and whistles. Being great at a few things often doesn't look all that flashy from afar. That's OK. You're aiming for a long-term relationship, not a one-night stand.

This is as true for advertising as it is for in-store packaging or displays. We've all seen a TV ad for some "revolutionary" gadget that will change your life. But when the actual product arrives in the mail, it turns out to be a disappointment. In-media good isn't nearly as important as at-home good. You can't paint over a bad experience with good advertising or marketing.

Don't write it down

How should you keep track of what customers want? Don't. Listen, but then forget what people said. Seriously.

There's no need for a spreadsheet, database, or filing system. The requests that really matter are the ones you'll hear over and over. After a while, you won't be able to forget them. Your customers will be your memory. They'll keep reminding you. They'll show you which things you truly need to worry about.

If there's a request that you keep forgetting, that's a sign that it isn't very important. The really important stuff doesn't go away.

CHAPTER

PROMOTION

WELCOME
OBSCURITY

Welcome obscurity

No one knows who you are right now. And that's just fine. Being obscure is a great position to be in. Be happy you're in the shadows.

Use this time to make mistakes without the whole world hearing about them. Keep tweaking. Work out the kinks. Test random ideas. Try new things. No one knows you, so it's no big deal if you mess up. Obscurity helps protect your ego and preserve your confidence.

Retailers experiment with test markets all the time for this reason. When Dunkin' Donuts thought about selling pizza, hot dogs, and other hot sandwiches, it test-marketed the products at just ten select locations.

Broadway shows also provide a great example of testing ideas on a small stage first. They routinely do a trial run in a smaller city before coming to New York. Testing out of town lets actors get some reps in front of a live audience before the show goes up in front of harsher critics and tastemakers.

Would you want the whole world to watch you the first time you do anything? If you've never given a speech before, do you want your first speech to be in front of ten thousand people or ten people? You don't want everyone to watch you *starting* your business. It makes no sense to tell everyone to look at you if you're not ready to be looked at yet.

And keep in mind that once you do get bigger and more popular, you're inevitably going to take fewer risks. When you're a success, the pressure to maintain predictability and consistency builds. You get more conservative. It's harder to take risks. That's when things start to fossilize and change becomes difficult.

If millions of people are using your product, every change you make will have a much bigger impact. Before, you might have upset a hundred people when you changed something. Now you might upset thousands. You can reason with a hundred people, but you need riot gear to deal with ten thousand angry customers.

These early days of obscurity are something you'll miss later on, when you're really under the microscope. Now's the time to take risks without worrying about embarrassing yourself.

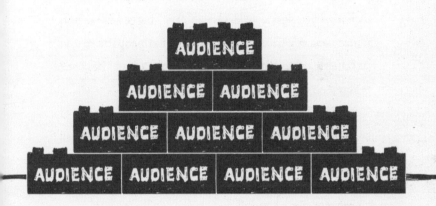

Build an audience

All companies have customers. Lucky companies have fans. But the most fortunate companies have *audiences*. An audience can be your secret weapon.

A lot of businesses still spend big bucks to reach people. Every time they want to say something, they dip into their budgets, pull out a huge wad of cash, and place some ads. But this approach is both expensive and unreliable. As they say, you waste half of your ad budget—you just don't know which half.

Today's smartest companies know better. Instead of going out to reach people, you want people to come to you. An audience returns often—on its own—to see what you have to say. This is the most receptive group of customers and potential customers you'll ever have.

Over the past ten years, we've built an audience of more than a hundred thousand daily readers for our Signal vs. Noise blog. Every day they come back to see what we have to say. We may talk about design or business or software or psychology or usability or our industry at large. Whatever it is, these people are interested enough to come back to hear more. And if they like what we have to say, they'll probably also like what we have to sell.

How much would it cost us to reach those hundred

thousand people every day the old-fashioned way? Hundreds of thousands? Millions? And how would we have done it? Running ads? Buying radio spots? Sending direct mail?

When you build an audience, you don't have to buy people's attention—they give it to you. This is a huge advantage.

So build an audience. Speak, write, blog, tweet, make videos—whatever. Share information that's valuable and you'll slowly but surely build a loyal audience. Then when you need to get the word out, the right people will already be listening.

don't

OUT-$PEND

OUT-TEACH

Out-teach your competition

You can advertise. You can hire salespeople. You can sponsor events. But your competitors are doing the same things. How does that help you stand out?

Instead of trying to outspend, outsell, or outsponsor competitors, try to out-teach them. Teaching probably isn't something your competitors are even thinking about. Most businesses focus on selling or servicing, but teaching never even occurs to them.

The Hoefler Type Foundry teaches designers about type at Typography.com. Etsy, an online store for things handmade, holds entrepreneurial workshops that explain "best practices" and promotional ideas to people who sell at the site. Gary Vaynerchuk, who owns a large wine shop, teaches people about wine online at Wine Library TV, and tens of thousands of people watch every day.

Teach and you'll form a bond you just don't get from traditional marketing tactics. Buying people's attention with a magazine or online banner ad is one thing. Earning their loyalty by teaching them forms a whole different connection. They'll trust you more. They'll respect you more. Even if they don't use your product, they can still be your fans.

Teaching is something individuals and small companies can do that bigger competitors can't. Big companies can afford a Super Bowl ad; you can't. But you can afford to teach, and that's something they'll never do, because big companies are obsessed with secrecy. Everything at those places has to get filtered through a lawyer and go through layers of red tape. Teaching is your chance to outmaneuver them.

Emulate chefs

You've probably heard of Emeril Lagasse, Mario Batali, Bobby Flay, Julia Child, Paula Deen, Rick Bayless, or Jacques Pépin. They're great chefs, but there are a lot of great chefs out there. So why do you know these few better than others? Because they share everything they know. They put their recipes in cookbooks and show their techniques on cooking shows.

As a business owner, you should share everything you know too. This is anathema to most in the business world. Businesses are usually paranoid and secretive. They think they have proprietary this and competitive advantage that. Maybe a rare few do, but most don't. And those that don't should stop acting like those that do. Don't be afraid of sharing.

A recipe is much easier to copy than a business. Shouldn't that scare Mario Batali? Why would he go on TV and show you how he does what he does? Why would he put all his recipes in cookbooks where anyone can buy and replicate them? Because he knows those recipes and techniques aren't enough to beat him at his own game. No one's going to buy his cookbook, open a restaurant next door, and put him out of business. It just doesn't work like that. Yet this is what many in the business world think will happen if their competitors learn how they do things. Get over it.

So emulate famous chefs. They cook, so they write cookbooks. What do you do? What are your "recipes"? What's your "cookbook"? What can you tell the world about how you operate that's informative, educational, and promotional? This book is our cookbook. What's yours?

Go behind the scenes

Give people a backstage pass and show them how your business works. Imagine that someone wanted to make a reality show about your business. What would they share? Now stop waiting for someone else and do it yourself.

Think no one will care? Think again. Even seemingly boring jobs can be fascinating when presented right. What could be more boring than commercial fishing and trucking? Yet the Discovery Channel and History Channel have turned these professions into highly rated shows: *Deadliest Catch* and *Ice Road Truckers*.

It doesn't need to be a dangerous job, either. People love finding out the little secrets of all kinds of businesses, even one that makes those tiny marshmallows in breakfast cereals. That's why the Food Network's *Unwrapped*—which explores the secrets behind lunch-box treats, soda pop, movie candy, and more—is such a popular program.

People are curious about how things are made. It's why they like factory tours or behind-the-scenes footage on DVDs. They want to see how the sets are built, how the animation is done, how the director cast the film, etc. They want to know how and why other people make decisions.

Letting people behind the curtain changes your relationship with them. They'll feel a bond with you and see you as human beings instead of a faceless company. They'll see the sweat and effort that goes into what you sell. They'll develop a deeper level of understanding and appreciation for what you do.

Nobody likes plastic flowers

The business world is full of "professionals" who wear the uniform and try to seem perfect. In truth, they just come off as stiff and boring. No one can relate to people like that.

Don't be afraid to show your flaws. Imperfections are real and people respond to real. It's why we like real flowers that wilt, not perfect plastic ones that never change. Don't worry about how you're supposed to sound and how you're supposed to act. Show the world what you're really like, warts and all.

There's a beauty to imperfection. This is the essence of the Japanese principle of *wabi-sabi*. *Wabi-sabi* values character and uniqueness over a shiny facade. It teaches that cracks and scratches in things should be embraced. It's also about simplicity. You strip things down and then use what you have. Leonard Koren, author of a book on *wabi-sabi,* gives this advice: Pare down to the essence, but don't remove the poetry. Keep things clean and unencumbered but don't sterilize.*

It's a beautiful way to put it: Leave the poetry in

---

*Pilar Viladas, "The Talk: The Slow Lane," *New York Times Magazine,* Oct. 9, 2005, www.tinyurl.com/ychqtup

what you make. When something becomes too pol-
ished, it loses its soul. It seems robotic.

So talk like you really talk. Reveal things that others
are unwilling to discuss. Be upfront about your short-
comings. Show the latest version of what you're working
on, even if you're not done yet. It's OK if it's not perfect.
You might not seem as professional, but you will seem a
lot more genuine.

Press releases are spam

What do you call a generic pitch sent out to hundreds of strangers hoping that one will bite? Spam. That's what press releases are too: generic pitches for coverage sent out to hundreds of journalists you don't know, hoping that one will write about you.

Let's dissect the purpose of a press release for a moment: It's something you send out because you want to be noticed. You want the press to pick up on your new company, product, service, announcement, or whatever. You want them to be excited enough to write a story about you.

But press releases are a terrible way to accomplish that. They're tired and formulaic. There's nothing exciting about them. Journalists sift through dozens a day. They wind up buried under an avalanche of hyperbolic headlines and fake quotes from CEOs. Everything is labeled sensational, revolutionary, groundbreaking, and amazing. It's numbing.

If you want to get someone's attention, it's silly to do exactly the same thing as everyone else. You need to stand out. So why issue press releases like everyone else does? Why spam journalists when their inbox is already filled with other people's spam?

Furthermore, a press release is generic. You write it

once and then send it to tons of reporters—people whom you don't know and who don't know you. And your first introduction is this vague, generic note you also send to everyone else? Is that the impression you want to make? Is that really going to get you the story?

Instead, call someone. Write a personal note. If you read a story about a similar company or product, contact the journalist who wrote it. Pitch her with some passion, some interest, some life. Do something meaningful. Be remarkable. Stand out. Be unforgettable. That's how you'll get the best coverage.

NICHE
MEDIA
OVER
MASS
MEDIA

Forget about the *Wall Street Journal*

Forget about *Time, Forbes, Newsweek, BusinessWeek,* the *New York Times,* and the *Wall Street Journal.* Pitching a reporter at one of these places is practically impossible. Good luck even getting ahold of that guy. And even if you do, he probably won't care anyway. You're not big enough to matter.

You're better off focusing on getting your story into a trade publication or picked up by a niche blogger. With these outlets, the barrier is much lower. You can send an e-mail and get a response (and maybe even a post) the same day. There's no editorial board or PR person involved. There's no pipeline your message has to go through.

These guys are actually hungry for fresh meat. They thrive on being tastemakers, finding the new thing, and getting the ball rolling. That's why many big-time reporters now use these smaller sites to find new stories. Stories that start on the fringe can go mainstream quickly.

We've been written up in big mainstream publications like *Wired* and *Time,* but we've found that we actually get more hits when we're profiled on sites like Daring Fireball, a site for Mac nerds, or Lifehacker, a productivity site. Links from these places result in notable spikes in our traffic and sales. Articles in big-time publications are nice, but they don't result in the same level of direct, instant activity.

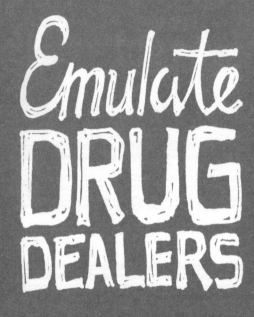

Emulate
DRUG
DEALERS

Drug dealers get it right

Drug dealers are astute businesspeople. They know their product is so good they're willing to give a little away for free upfront. They know you'll be back for more—with money.

Emulate drug dealers. Make your product so good, so addictive, so "can't miss" that giving customers a small, free taste makes them come back with cash in hand.

This will force you to make something about your product bite-size. You want an easily digestible introduction to what you sell. This gives people a way to try it without investing any money or a lot of time.

Bakeries, restaurants, and ice cream shops have done this successfully for years. Car dealers let you test-drive cars before buying them. Software firms are also getting on board, with free trials or limited-use versions. How many other industries could benefit from the drug-dealer model?

Don't be afraid to give a little away for free—as long as you've got something else to sell. Be confident in what you're offering. You should know that people will come back for more. If you're not confident about that, you haven't created a strong enough product.

Marketing is not a department

Do you have a marketing department? If not, good. If you do, don't think these are the only people responsible for marketing. Accounting is a department. Marketing isn't. Marketing is something everyone in your company is doing 24/7/365.

Just as you cannot not communicate, you cannot not market:

- Every time you answer the phone, it's marketing.
- Every time you send an e-mail, it's marketing.
- Every time someone uses your product, it's marketing.
- Every word you write on your Web site is marketing.
- If you build software, every error message is marketing.
- If you're in the restaurant business, the after-dinner mint is marketing.
- If you're in the retail business, the checkout counter is marketing.
- If you're in a service business, your invoice is marketing.

Recognize that all of these little things are more important than choosing which piece of swag to throw into a conference goodie bag. Marketing isn't just a few individual events. It's the sum total of everything you do.

The myth of the overnight sensation

You will not be a big hit right away. You will not get rich quick. You are not so special that everyone else will instantly pay attention. No one cares about you. At least not yet. Get used to it.

You know those overnight-success stories you've heard about? It's not the whole story. Dig deeper and you'll usually find people who have busted their asses for years to get into a position where things could take off. And on the rare occasion that instant success does come along, it usually doesn't last—there's no foundation there to support it.

Trade the dream of overnight success for slow, measured growth. It's hard, but you have to be patient. You have to grind it out. You have to do it for a long time before the right people notice.

You may think you can speed up the process by hiring a PR firm. Don't bother. You're just not ready for that yet. For one thing, it's too expensive. Good PR firms can cost upward of $10,000 per month. That's a waste of money right now.

Plus, you're still just a no-name with a product no one's ever heard about. Who's going to write about that? Once you have some customers and a history, you'll have a story to tell. But just launching isn't a good story.

And remember, great brands launch without PR campaigns all the time. Starbucks, Apple, Nike, Amazon, Google, and Snapple all became great brands over time, not because of a big PR push upfront.

Start building your audience today. Start getting people interested in what you have to say. And then keep at it. In a few years, you too will get to chuckle when people discuss your "overnight" success.

CHAPTER

HIRING

Do it yourself first

Never hire anyone to do a job until you've tried to do it yourself first. That way, you'll understand the nature of the work. You'll know what a job well done looks like. You'll know how to write a realistic job description and which questions to ask in an interview. You'll know whether to hire someone full-time or part-time, outsource it, or keep doing it yourself (the last is preferable, if possible).

You'll also be a much better manager, because you'll be supervising people who are doing a job you've done before. You'll know when to criticize and when to support.

At 37signals, we didn't hire a system administrator until one of us had spent a whole summer setting up a bunch of servers on his own. For the first three years, one of us did all of our customer support. Then we hired a dedicated support person. We ran with the ball as far as we could before handing it off. That way, we knew what we were looking for once we did decide to hire.

You may feel out of your element at times. You might even feel like you suck. That's all right. You can hire your way out of that feeling or you can learn your way out of it. Try learning first. What you give up in initial execution will be repaid many times over by the wisdom you gain.

Plus, you should want to be intimately involved in all aspects of your business. Otherwise you'll wind up in the dark, putting your fate solely in the hands of others. That's dangerous.

Hire when it hurts

Don't hire for pleasure; hire to kill pain. Always ask yourself: What if we don't hire anyone? Is that extra work that's burdening us really necessary? Can we solve the problem with a slice of software or a change of practice instead? What if we just don't do it?

Similarly, if you lose someone, don't replace him immediately. See how long you can get by without that person and that position. You'll often discover you don't need as many people as you think.

The right time to hire is when there's more work than you can handle for a sustained period of time. There should be things you can't do anymore. You should notice the quality level slipping. That's when you're hurting. And that's when it's time to hire, not earlier.

Pass on great people

Some companies are addicted to hiring. Some even hire when they aren't hiring. They'll hear about someone great and invent a position or title just to lure them in. And there they'll sit—parked in a position that doesn't matter, doing work that isn't important.

Pass on hiring people you don't need, even if you think that person's a great catch. You'll be doing your company more harm than good if you bring in talented people who have nothing important to do.

Problems start when you have more people than you need. You start inventing work to keep everyone busy. Artificial work leads to artificial projects. And those artificial projects lead to real costs and complexity.

Don't worry about "the one that got away." It's much worse to have people on staff who aren't doing anything meaningful. There's plenty of talent out there. When you do have a real need, you'll find someone who fits well.

Great has nothing to do with it. If you don't need someone, you don't need someone.

Strangers at a cocktail party

If you go to a cocktail party where everyone is a stranger, the conversation is dull and stiff. You make small talk about the weather, sports, TV shows, etc. You shy away from serious conversations and controversial opinions.

A small, intimate dinner party among old friends is a different story, though. There are genuinely interesting conversations and heated debates. At the end of the night, you feel you actually got something out of it.

Hire a ton of people rapidly and a "strangers at a cocktail party" problem is exactly what you end up with. There are always new faces around, so everyone is unfailingly polite. Everyone tries to avoid any conflict or drama. No one says, "This idea sucks." People appease instead of challenge.

And that appeasement is what gets companies into trouble. You need to be able to tell people when they're full of crap. If that doesn't happen, you start churning out something that doesn't offend anyone but also doesn't make anyone fall in love.

You need an environment where everyone feels safe enough to be honest when things get tough. You need to know how far you can push someone. You need to know what people really mean when they say something.

So hire slowly. It's the only way to avoid winding up at a cocktail party of strangers.

Resumés are ridiculous

We all know resumés are a joke. They're exaggerations. They're filled with "action verbs" that don't mean anything. They list job titles and responsibilities that are vaguely accurate at best. And there's no way to verify most of what's on there. The whole thing is a farce.

Worst of all, they're too easy. Anyone can create a decent-enough resumé. That's why half-assed applicants love them so much. They can shotgun out hundreds at a time to potential employers. It's another form of spam. They don't care about landing *your* job; they just care about landing *any* job.

If someone sends out a resumé to three hundred companies, that's a huge red flag right there. There's no way that applicant has researched you. There's no way he knows what's different about your company.

If you hire based on this garbage, you're missing the point of what hiring is about. You want a specific candidate who cares specifically about your company, your products, your customers, and your job.

So how do you find these candidates? First step: Check the cover letter. In a cover letter, you get actual communication instead of a list of skills, verbs, and years of irrelevance. There's no way an applicant can churn out hundreds of personalized letters. That's why the cover letter is a much better test than a resumé. You hear someone's actual voice and are able recognize if it's in tune with you and your company.

Trust your gut reaction. If the first paragraph sucks, the second has to work that much harder. If there's no hook in the first three, it's unlikely there's a match there. On the other hand, if your gut is telling you there's a chance at a real match, then move on to the interview stage.

WHAT DOES

5

YEARS

EXPERIENCE
MEAN *anyway?*

Years of irrelevance

We've all seen job ads that say, "Five years of experience required." That may give you a number, but it tells you nothing.

Of course, requiring some baseline level of experience can be a good idea when hiring. It makes sense to go after candidates with six months to a year of experience. It takes that long to internalize the idioms, learn how things work, understand the relevant tools, etc.

But after that, the curve flattens out. There's surprisingly little difference between a candidate with six months of experience and one with six years. The real difference comes from the individual's dedication, personality, and intelligence.

How do you really measure this stuff anyway? What does five years of experience mean? If you spent a couple of weekends experimenting with something a few years back, can you count that as a year of experience? How is a company supposed to verify these claims? These are murky waters.

How long someone's been doing it is overrated. What matters is how *well* they've been doing it.

Forget about formal education

*I have never let my schooling
interfere with my education.*
—MARK TWAIN

There are plenty of companies out there who have educational requirements. They'll only hire people with a
college degree (sometimes in a specific field) or an ad-
vanced degree or a certain GPA or certification of some
sort or some other requirement.

Come on. There are plenty of intelligent people
who don't excel in the classroom. Don't fall into the trap
of thinking you need someone from one of the "best"
schools in order to get results. Ninety percent of CEOs
currently heading the top five hundred American companies did not receive undergraduate degrees from Ivy
League colleges. In fact, more received their undergraduate degrees from the University of Wisconsin than
from Harvard (the most heavily represented Ivy school,
with nine CEOs).*

---

*Carol Hymowitz, "Any College Will Do," *Wall Street Journal,* Sept.
18, 2006, online.wsj.com/article/SB115853818747665842.html

Too much time in academia can actually do you harm. Take writing, for example. When you get out of school, you have to unlearn so much of the way they teach you to write there. Some of the misguided lessons you learn in academia:

- The longer a document is, the more it matters.
- Stiff, formal tone is better than being conversational.
- Using big words is impressive.
- You need to write a certain number of words or pages to make a point.
- The format matters as much (or more) than the content of what you write.

It's no wonder so much business writing winds up dry, wordy, and dripping with nonsense. People are just continuing the bad habits they picked up in school. It's not just academic writing, either. There are a lot of skills that are useful in academia that aren't worth much outside of it.

Bottom line: The pool of great candidates is far bigger than just people who completed college with a stellar GPA. Consider dropouts, people who had low GPAs, community-college students, and even those who just went to high school.

DELEGATORS
ARE
DEAD
WEIGHT

Everybody works

With a small team, you need people who are going to *do* work, not delegate work. Everyone's got to be producing. No one can be above the work.

That means you need to avoid hiring delegators, those people who love telling others what to do. Delegators are dead weight for a small team. They clog the pipes for others by coming up with busywork. And when they run out of work to assign, they make up more—regardless of whether it needs to be done.

Delegators love to pull people into meetings, too. In fact, meetings are a delegator's best friend. That's where he gets to seem important. Meanwhile, everyone else who attends is pulled away from getting real work done.

HIRE MANAGERS of 1

Hire managers of one

Managers of one are people who come up with their own goals and execute them. They don't need heavy direction. They don't need daily check-ins. They do what a manager would do—set the tone, assign items, determine what needs to get done, etc.—but they do it by themselves and for themselves.

These people free you from oversight. They set their own direction. When you leave them alone, they surprise you with how much they've gotten done. They don't need a lot of hand-holding or supervision.

How can you spot these people? Look at their backgrounds. They have set the tone for how they've worked at other jobs. They've run something on their own or launched some kind of project.

You want someone who's capable of building something from scratch and seeing it through. Finding these people frees the rest of your team to work more and manage less.

222

Hire great writers

If you are trying to decide among a few people to fill a position, hire the best writer. It doesn't matter if that person is a marketer, salesperson, designer, programmer, or whatever; their writing skills will pay off.

That's because being a good writer is about more than writing. Clear writing is a sign of clear thinking. Great writers know how to communicate. They make things easy to understand. They can put themselves in someone else's shoes. They know what to omit. And those are qualities you want in any candidate.

Writing is making a comeback all over our society. Look at how much people e-mail and text-message now rather than talk on the phone. Look at how much communication happens via instant messaging and blogging. Writing is today's currency for good ideas.

THE BEST ARE

EVERYWHERE

The best are everywhere

It's crazy not to hire the best people just because they live far away. Especially now that there's so much technology out there making it easier to bring everyone together online.

Our headquarters are in Chicago, but more than half of our team lives elsewhere. We've got people in Spain, Canada, Idaho, Oklahoma, and elsewhere. Had we limited our search only to people in Chicago, we would have missed out on half of the great people we have.

To make sure your remote team stays in touch, have at least a few hours a day of real-time overlap. Working in time zones where there's no workday overlap at all is tough. If you face that situation, someone might need to shift hours a bit so they start a little later or earlier in the day, so you're available at the same time. You don't need eight hours of overlap, though. (Actually, we've found it preferable to *not* have complete overlap—you get more alone time that way.) Two to four hours of overlap should be plenty.

Also, meet in person once in a while. You should see each other at least every few months. We make sure our whole team gets together a few times a year. These are great times to review progress, discuss what's going right or wrong, plan for the future, and get reacquainted with one another on a personal level.

Geography just doesn't matter anymore. Hire the best talent, regardless of where it is.

Test-drive employees

Interviews are only worth so much. Some people sound like pros but don't work like pros. You need to evaluate the work they can do now, not the work they say they did in the past.

The best way to do that is to actually see them work. Hire them for a miniproject, even if it's for just twenty or forty hours. You'll see how they make decisions. You'll see if you get along. You'll see what kind of questions they ask. You'll get to judge them by their actions instead of just their words.

You can even make up a fake project. In a factory in South Carolina, BMW built a simulated assembly line where job candidates get ninety minutes to perform a variety of work-related tasks.*

Cessna, the airplane manufacturer, has a role-playing exercise for prospective managers that simulates the day of an executive. Candidates work through memos, deal with (phony) irate customers, and handle other problems. Cessna has hired more than a hundred people using this simulation.†

---

*Peter Carbonara, "Hire for Attitude, Train for Skill," *Fast Company*, Dec. 18, 2007,
www.fastcompany.com/magazine/04/hiring.html
†Ibid.

These companies have realized that when you get into a real work environment, the truth comes out. It's one thing to look at a portfolio, read a resumé, or conduct an interview. It's another to actually work with someone.

DAMAGE CONTROL

Own your bad news

When something goes wrong, someone is going to tell the story. You'll be better off if it's you. Otherwise, you create an opportunity for rumors, hearsay, and false information to spread.

When something bad happens, tell your customers (even if they never noticed in the first place). Don't think you can just sweep it under the rug. You can't hide anymore. These days, someone else will call you on it if you don't do it yourself. They'll post about it online and everyone will know. There are no more secrets.

People will respect you more if you are open, honest, public, and responsive during a crisis. Don't hide behind spin or try to keep your bad news on the down low. You want your customers to be as informed as possible.

Back in 1989, the *Exxon Valdez* oil tanker spilled 11 million gallons of oil into Alaska's Prince William Sound. Exxon made the mistake of waiting a long time before responding to the spill and sending aid to Alaska. Exxon's chairman failed to go there until two weeks after the spill. The company held news briefings in Valdez, a remote Alaskan town that was difficult for the press to reach. The result: a PR disaster for Exxon that led the public to believe the company was either hiding something or didn't really care about what had happened.*

Contrast that Exxon story to the rupture of an Ashland Oil storage tank that spilled oil into a river near Pittsburgh around the same time. Ashland Oil's chairman, John Hall, went to the scene of the Ashland spill and took charge. He pledged to clean everything up. He visited news bureaus to explain what the company would do and answer any questions. Within a day, he had shifted the story from a rotten-oil-company-does-evil narrative to a good-oil-company-tries-to-clean-up story.†

Here are some tips on how you can own the story:

- The message should come from the top. The highest-ranking person available should take control in a forceful way.
- Spread the message far and wide. Use whatever megaphone you have. Don't try to sweep it under the rug.

---

*Reyna Susi, "The Exxon Crisis, 1989," Effective Crisis Management, iml.jou.ufl.edu/projects/Fall02/Susi/exxon.htm
†John Holusha, "Exxon's Public-Relations Problem," *New York Times*, Apr. 21, 1989, www.tinyurl.com/yg2bgff

- "No comment" is not an option.
- Apologize the way a real person would and explain what happened in detail.
- Honestly be concerned about the fate of your customers—then prove it.

Speed changes everything

"Your call is very important to us. We appreciate your patience. The average hold time right now is sixteen minutes." Give me a fucking break.

Getting back to people quickly is probably the most important thing you can do when it comes to customer service. It's amazing how much that can defuse a bad situation and turn it into a good one.

Have you ever sent an e-mail and it took days or weeks for the company to get back to you? How did it make you feel? These days, that's what people have come to expect. They're used to being put on hold. They're used to platitudes about "caring" that aren't backed up.

That's why so many support queries start off with an antagonistic tone. Some people may even make threats or call you names. Don't take it personally. They think that's the only way to be heard. They're only trying to be a squeaky wheel in hopes it'll get them a little grease.

Once you answer quickly, they shift 180 degrees. They light up. They become extra polite. Often they thank you profusely.

It's especially true if you offer a personal response. Customers are so used to canned answers, you can really differentiate yourself by answering thoughtfully and showing that you're listening. And even if you don't have a perfect answer, say something. "Let me do some research and get back to you" can work wonders.

How to say you're sorry

There's never really a great way to say you're sorry, but there are plenty of terrible ways.

One of the worst ways is the non-apology apology, which sounds like an apology but doesn't really accept any blame. For example, "We're sorry if this upset you." Or "I'm sorry that you don't feel we lived up to your expectations." Whatever.

A good apology accepts responsibility. It has no conditional *if* phrase attached. It shows people that the buck stops with you. And then it provides real details about what happened and what you're doing to prevent it from happening again. And it seeks a way to make things right.

Here's another bad one: "We apologize for any inconvenience this may have caused." Oh, please. Let's break down why that's bad:

"We apologize . . ." If you spilled coffee on someone while riding the subway, would you say, "I apologize"? No, you'd say, "I'm so, so sorry!" Well, if your service is critical to your customers, an interruption to that service is like spilling hot coffee all over them. So use the appropriate tone and language to show that you understand the severity of what happened. Also, the person in charge should take personal responsibility. An "I" apology is a lot stronger than a "we" apology.

" . . . **any inconvenience . . .**" If customers depend on your service and can't get to it, it's not merely an inconvenience. It's a crisis. An inconvenience is a long line at the grocery store. This ain't that.

" . . . **this may have caused**" The "may" here implies there might not be *anything* wrong at all. That's a classic non-apology apology move. It slights the very real problem(s) that customers are experiencing. If this didn't affect them, you don't really need to say anything. If it did affect them, then there's no need for "may" here. Stop wavering.

So what's the perfect way to say you're sorry? There's no magic bullet. Any stock answer will sound generic and hollow. You're going to have to take it on a case-by-case basis.

The number-one principle to keep in mind when you apologize: How would you feel about the apology if you were on the other end? If someone said those words to you, would you believe them?

Keep in mind that you can't apologize your way out of being an ass. Even the best apology won't rescue you if you haven't earned people's trust. Everything you do before things go wrong matters far more than the actual words you use to apologize. If you've built rapport with customers, they'll cut you some slack and trust you when you say you're sorry.

Put everyone on the front lines

In the restaurant business, there's a world of difference between working in the kitchen and dealing with customers. Cooking schools and smart restaurateurs know it's important for both sides to understand and empathize with each other. That's why they often have chefs work out front as waiters for a stretch. That way, the kitchen staff can interact with customers and see what it's actually like on the front lines.

A lot of companies have a similar front-of-house/ back-of-house split. The people who make the product work in the "kitchen" while support handles the customers. Unfortunately, that means the product's chefs never get to directly hear what customers are saying. Too bad. Listening to customers is the best way to get in tune with a product's strengths and weaknesses.

Think about the children's game Telephone. There are ten kids sitting in a circle. A message starts and is whispered from one child to another. By the time it gets all the way around, the message is completely distorted—to the point where it's usually hilarious. A sentence that makes sense at first comes out the other end as "Macaroni cantaloupe knows the future." And the more people you have in the circle, the more distorted the message gets.

The same thing is true at your company. The more people you have between your customers' words and the people doing the work, the more likely it is that the message will get lost or distorted along the way.

Everyone on your team should be connected to your customers—maybe not every day, but at least a few times throughout the year. That's the only way your team is going to feel the hurt your customers are experiencing. It's feeling the hurt that really motivates people to fix the problem. And the flip side is true too: The joy of happy customers or ones who have had a problem solved can also be wildly motivating.

So don't protect the people doing the work from customer feedback. No one should be shielded from direct criticism.

Maybe you think you don't have time to interact with customers. Then make time. Craigslist founder Craig Newmark still answers support e-mails today (often within minutes). He also deletes racist comments from the site's discussion boards and pesters New York City Realtors who post apartments for rent that don't exist.* If he can devote this kind of attention to customer service, you can too.

---

*Scott Kirsner, "Craigslist's Unorthodox Path," *Boston Globe,* June 15, 2008, www.tinyurl.com/4vkg58

Take a deep breath

When you rock the boat, there will be waves. After you introduce a new feature, change a policy, or remove something, knee-jerk reactions will pour in. Resist the urge to panic or make rapid changes in response. Passions flare in the beginning. That's normal. But if you ride out that first rocky week, things usually settle down.

People are creatures of habit. That's why they react to change in such a negative way. They're used to using something in a certain way and any change upsets the natural order of things. So they push back. They complain. They demand that you revert to the way things were.

But that doesn't mean you should act. Sometimes you need to go ahead with a decision you believe in, even if it's unpopular at first.

People often respond before they give a change a fair chance. Sometimes that initial negative reaction is more of a primal response. That's why you'll sometimes hear things like, "It's the worst thing I've ever seen." No, it's not. It's a minor change. Come on.

Also, remember that negative reactions are almost always louder and more passionate than positive ones. In fact, you may hear only negative voices even when the majority of your customers are happy about a change. Make sure you don't foolishly backpedal on a necessary but controversial decision.

So when people complain, let things simmer for a while. Let them know you're listening. Show them you're aware of what they're saying. Let them know you understand their discontent. But explain that you're going to let it go for a while and see what happens. You'll probably find that people will adjust eventually. They may even wind up liking the change more than the old way, once they get used to it.

CHAPTER

CULTURE

CULTURE IS THE BY-PRODUCT of CONSISTENT BEHAVIOR

You don't create a culture

Instant cultures are artificial cultures. They're big bangs made of mission statements, declarations, and rules. They are obvious, ugly, and plastic. Artificial culture is paint. Real culture is patina.

You don't create a culture. It happens. This is why new companies don't have a culture. Culture is the by-product of consistent behavior. If you encourage people to share, then sharing will be built into your culture. If you reward trust, then trust will be built in. If you treat customers right, then treating customers right becomes your culture.

Culture isn't a foosball table or trust falls. It isn't policy. It isn't the Christmas party or the company picnic. Those are objects and events, not culture. And it's not a slogan, either. Culture is action, not words.

So don't worry too much about it. Don't force it. You can't install a culture. Like a fine scotch, you've got to give it time to develop.

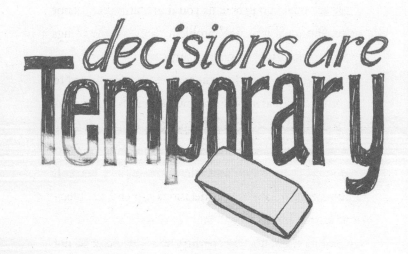

decisions are
Temporary

Decisions are temporary

"But what if . . . ?" "What happens when . . . ?" "Don't we need to plan for . . . ?"

Don't make up problems you don't have yet. It's not a problem until it's a *real* problem. Most of the things you worry about never happen anyway.

Besides, the decisions you make today don't need to last forever. It's easy to shoot down good ideas, interesting policies, or worthwhile experiments by assuming that whatever you decide now needs to work for years on end. It's just not so, especially for a small business. If circumstances change, your decisions can change. Decisions are temporary.

At this stage, it's silly to worry about whether or not your concept will scale from five to five thousand people (or from a hundred thousand to 100 million people). Getting a product or service off the ground is hard enough without inventing even more obstacles. Optimize for now and worry about the future later.

The ability to change course is one of the big advantages of being small. Compared with larger competitors, you're way more capable of making quick, sweeping changes. Big companies just can't move that fast. So pay attention to today and worry about later when it gets here. Otherwise you'll waste energy, time, and money fixating on problems that may never materialize.

BUILD A ROCKSTAR ENVIRONMENT

Skip the rock stars

A lot of companies post help-wanted ads seeking "rock stars" or "ninjas." Lame. Unless your workplace is filled with groupies and throwing stars, these words have nothing to do with your business.

Instead of thinking about how you can land a roomful of rock stars, think about the room instead. We're all capable of bad, average, and great work. The environment has a lot more to do with great work than most people realize.

That's not to say we're all created equal and you'll unlock star power in anyone with a rockstar environment. But there's a ton of untapped potential trapped under lame policies, poor direction, and stifling bureaucracies. Cut the crap and you'll find that people are waiting to do great work. They just need to be given the chance.

This isn't about casual Fridays or bring-your-dog-to-work day. (If those are such good things, then why aren't you doing them every day of the week?)

Rockstar environments develop out of trust, autonomy, and responsibility. They're a result of giving people the privacy, workspace, and tools they deserve. Great environments show respect for the people who do the work and how they do it.

They're not thirteen

When you treat people like children, you get children's work. Yet that's exactly how a lot of companies and managers treat their employees. Employees need to ask permission before they can do anything. They need to get approval for every tiny expenditure. It's surprising they don't have to get a hall pass to go take a shit.

When everything constantly needs approval, you create a culture of nonthinkers. You create a boss-versus-worker relationship that screams, "I don't trust you."

What do you gain if you ban employees from, say, visiting a social-networking site or watching YouTube while at work? You gain nothing. That time doesn't magically convert to work. They'll just find some other diversion.

And look, you're not going to get a full eight hours a day out of people anyway. That's a myth. They might be at the office for eight hours, but they're not actually working eight hours. People *need* diversions. It helps disrupt the monotony of the workday. A little YouTube or Facebook time never hurt anyone.

Then there's all the money and time you spend policing this stuff. How much does it cost to set up surveillance software? How much time do IT employees waste on monitoring other employees instead of working on a project that's actually valuable? How much time do you waste writing rule books that never get read? Look at the costs and you quickly realize that failing to trust your employees is awfully expensive.

SEND PEOPLE HOME at FIVE

Send people home at 5

The dream employee for a lot of companies is a twenty-something with as little of a life as possible outside of work—someone who'll be fine working fourteen-hour days and sleeping under his desk.

But packing a room full of these burn-the-midnight-oil types isn't as great as it seems. It lets you get away with lousy execution. It perpetuates myths like "This is the only way we can compete against the big guys." You don't need more hours; you need *better* hours.

When people have something to do at home, they get down to business. They get their work done at the office because they have somewhere else to be. They find ways to be more efficient because they have to. They need to pick up the kids or get to choir practice. So they use their time wisely.

As the saying goes, "If you want something done, ask the busiest person you know." You want busy people. People who have a life outside of work. People who care about more than one thing. You shouldn't expect the job to be someone's entire life—at least not if you want to keep them around for a long time.

Don't scar on the first cut

The second something goes wrong, the natural tendency is to create a policy. "Someone's wearing shorts!? We need a dress code!" No, you don't. You just need to tell John not to wear shorts again.

Policies are organizational scar tissue. They are codified overreactions to situations that are unlikely to happen again. They are collective punishment for the misdeeds of an individual.

This is how bureaucracies are born. No one sets out to create a bureaucracy. They sneak up on companies slowly. They are created one policy—one scar—at a time.

So don't scar on the first cut. Don't create a policy because one person did something wrong once. Policies are only meant for situations that come up over and over again.

Sound like you

What is it with businesspeople trying to sound big? The stiff language, the formal announcements, the artificial friendliness, the legalese, etc. You read this stuff and it sounds like a robot wrote it. These companies talk *at* you, not *to* you.

This mask of professionalism is a joke. We all know this. Yet small companies still try to emulate it. They think sounding big makes them appear bigger and more "professional." But it really just makes them sound ridiculous. Plus, you sacrifice one of a small company's greatest assets: the ability to communicate simply and directly, without running every last word through a legal- and PR-department sieve.

There's nothing wrong with sounding your own size. Being honest about who you are is smart business, too. Language is often your first impression—why start it off with a lie? Don't be afraid to be you.

That applies to the language you use everywhere—in e-mail, packaging, interviews, blog posts, presentations, etc. Talk to customers the way you would to friends. Explain things as if you were sitting next to them. Avoid jargon or any sort of corporate-speak. Stay away from buzzwords when normal words will do just fine. Don't talk about "monetization" or being "transparent"; talk about making money and being honest. Don't use seven words when four will do.

And don't force your employees to end e-mails with legalese like "This e-mail message is for the sole use of the intended recipient(s) and may contain confidential and privileged information." That's like ending all your company e-mails with a signature that says, "We don't trust you and we're ready to prove it in court." Good luck making friends that way.

Write to be read, don't write just to write. Whenever you write something, read it out loud. Does it sound the way it would if you were actually talking to someone? If not, how can you make it more conversational?

Who said writing needs to be formal? Who said you have to strip away your personality when putting words on paper? Forget rules. Communicate!

And when you're writing, don't think about all the people who may read your words. Think of one person. Then write for that one person. Writing for a mob leads to generalities and awkwardness. When you write to a specific target, you're a lot more likely to hit the mark.

Four-letter words

There are four-letter words you should never use in business. They're not *fuck* or *shit*. They're *need, must, can't, easy, just, only,* and *fast*. These words get in the way of healthy communication. They are red flags that introduce animosity, torpedo good discussions, and cause projects to be late.

When you use these four-letter words, you create a black-and-white situation. But the truth is rarely black and white. So people get upset and problems ensue. Tension and conflict are injected unnecessarily.

Here's what's wrong with some of them:

Need. Very few things actually need to get done. Instead of saying "need," you're better off saying "maybe" or "What do you think about this?" or "How does this sound?" or "Do you think we could get away with that?"

Can't. When you say "can't," you probably can. Sometimes there are even opposing can'ts: "We can't launch it like that, because it's not quite right" versus "We can't spend any more time on this because we have to launch." Both of those statements can't be true. Or wait a minute, can they?

Easy. *Easy* is a word that's used to describe other people's jobs. "That should be easy for you to do, right?" But notice how rarely people describe their own tasks as easy. For you, it's "Let me look into it"—but for others, it's "Get it done."

These four-letter words often pop up during debates (and also watch out for their cousins: *everyone, no one, always,* and *never*). Once uttered, they make it tough to find a solution. They box you into a corner by pitting two absolutes against each other. That's when head-butting occurs. You squeeze out any middle ground.

And these words are especially dangerous when you string them together: "We need to add this feature now. We can't launch without this feature. Everyone wants it. It's only one little thing so it will be easy. You should be able to get it in there fast!" Only thirty-six words, but a hundred assumptions. That's a recipe for disaster.

ASAP is poison

Stop saying ASAP. We get it. It's implied. Everyone wants things done as soon as they can be done.

When you turn into one of these people who adds ASAP to the end of every request, you're saying everything is high priority. And when everything is high priority, nothing is. (Funny how everything is a top priority until you actually have to prioritize things.)

ASAP is inflationary. It devalues any request that doesn't say ASAP. Before you know it, the only way to get anything done is by putting the ASAP sticker on it.

Most things just don't warrant that kind of hysteria. If a task doesn't get done this very instant, nobody is going to die. Nobody's going to lose their job. It won't cost the company a ton of money. What it will do is create artificial stress, which leads to burnout and worse.

So reserve your use of emergency language for true emergencies. The kind where there are direct, measurable consequences to inaction. For everything else, chill out.

CHAPTER

CONCLUSION

Inspiration is perishable

We all have ideas. Ideas are immortal. They last forever.

What doesn't last forever is inspiration. Inspiration is like fresh fruit or milk: It has an expiration date.

If you want to do something, you've got to do it now. You can't put it on a shelf and wait two months to get around to it. You can't just say you'll do it later. Later, you won't be pumped up about it anymore.

If you're inspired on a Friday, swear off the weekend and dive into the project. When you're high on inspiration, you can get two weeks of work done in twenty-four hours. Inspiration is a time machine in that way.

Inspiration is a magical thing, a productivity multiplier, a motivator. But it won't wait for you. Inspiration is a now thing. If it grabs you, grab it right back and put it to work.

Thank you for reading our book

We hope it inspires you to rework how you do things. If so, drop a line to rework@37signals.com and let us know how it's going. We look forward to hearing from you.

CHAPTER

RESOURCES

About 37signals

37signals
www.37signals.com
About 37signals and our products.

Rework site
www.37signals.com/rework
The official book site.

Signal vs. Noise
www.37signals.com/svn
Our company blog about business, design, culture, and more.

37signals video
www.37signals.com/speaks
Presentations and rants by 37signals.

Subscribe to 37signals newsletters
www.37signals.com/subscribe
Newsletter about new products, discounts, and more (sent out roughly twice a month).

Stuff we like
www.37signals.com/stuffwelike
A list of books, sites, and other things that we enjoy.

E-mail
rework@37signals.com

37signals products

Basecamp
www.basecamphq.com
Manage projects and collaborate with your team and clients.

Highrise
www.highrisehq.com
Track your contacts, leads, and deals. Always be prepared.

Backpack
www.backpackit.com
Organize and share information across your business.

Campfire
www.campfirenow.com
Real-time chat and file and code sharing for remote teams.

Ta-da List
www.tadalist.com
Ta-da List makes it easy to create and share your to-do's.

Writeboard
www.writeboard.com
Writeboard is a collaborative writing tool.

Getting Real
gettingreal.37signals.com
This book by 37signals will help you discover the smarter, faster, easier way to build a successful Web-based application.

Ruby on Rails
www.rubyonrails.org
An open-source Web framework created by 37signals.

Acknowledgments

Very special thanks go to Matthew Linderman. Matt was 37signals' first employee in 1999—and he's still with the company today. This book wouldn't have come together without Matt. In addition to writing original content, he helped merge the distinctly different writing styles of the coauthors into a focused, cohesive book. He made it look easy, but it wasn't easy work. Thank you, Matt.

We also want to thank our families, our customers, and everyone at 37signals. And here's a list of some of the people we know, and don't know, who have sinpired us in one way or another:

Frank Lloyd Wright
Warren Buffett
Clayton Christensen
Jim Coudal
Ernest Kim
Scott Heiferman
Carlos Segura
Steve Jobs
Bill Maher
Mies van der Rohe
Christopher Alexander
Kent Beck
Gerald Weinberg
Julia Child
Nicholas Karavites
Richard Bird
Dieter Rams
Ron Paul

Seth Godin
Jamie Larson
Ralph Nader
Benjamin Franklin
Jeff Bezos
Antoni Gaudi
Larry David
Dean Kamen
Thomas Jefferson
Ricardo Semler
James Dyson
Thomas Paine
Kathy Sierra
Marc Hedlund
Michael Jordan
Jeffrey Zeldman
Judith Sheindlin
Timothy Ferriss